RAFAEL BIOGRAPHY

The King of Clay -Journey of a Tennis Legend

Ryan Keith Bestwick

-Biography-

RAFAEL NADAL

The King of Clay—Journey of a Tennis Legend

CONTENTS

INTRODUCTION

He described himself as being "physically destroyed." Emotions were running high as well. He was so high that he couldn't sleep the night following the match.

"I feel lucky to have achieved one more very special thing in my tennis career," he said after earning his 21st Grand Slam trophy. "I don't care if I'm the one or if I'm not the one; if I'm the best in history or if I'm not the best in history."

But that was simply my modesty speaking. The bright smile on his face revealed that he is eager to win the battle with Roger Federer and Novak Djokovic to be the greatest of all time.

Congratulations flooded in from everywhere. "A final of Herculean proportions," Australian tennis legend Rod Laver said as he handed the trophy to the Spaniard. "Given everything you've been through, this historic victory is so special, Rafa; it's been a pleasure to watch you accomplish what you love."

Billie Jean King, the former American champion, was equally taken aback. "The mental and physical marathon of a five-hour Grand Slam final requires grit, guts, spirit, and determination," she says. "What an amazing comeback!" Federer was clearly taken aback by his opponent. "What a match!" remarked him. "My heartfelt congratulations to my friend and great rival, Roger Federer, on becoming the first man to win 21 Grand Slam singles titles." Amazing. Never underestimate the power of a great champion. Your incredible work ethic, dedication, and fighting spirit inspire me and millions of others around the world."

CHAPTER 1

EARLY YEARS

"I lost to him during an exhibition match. He was 14 years old, but I took heart by thinking that I had lost to a future Roland Garros champion."

1987 Wimbledon champion Pat Cash

Rafa used to accompany his uncle to Real Mallorca's home field in Palma as a child, and once, at the age of ten, accompanied him to FC Barcelona's Camp Nou stadium to join in with the other team players after a training session. All of this meant that the Nadal family was used to having a sports hero in their midst, which may explain why they seemed unconcerned by Rafa's later success. Sport, primarily football or tennis, filled the majority of Rafa's youth. He was kicking enormous, white balls at the local Manacor football club when he wasn't striking yellow balls at Club Tenis Manacor. He was a self-professed football aficionado who aspired to be a professional player. At the age of 11, he helped his young team win the Balearic Islands tournament, describing the thrill he felt as equal to the elation he had years later when he won a tennis Grand Slam title.

Meanwhile, Toni and his tutoring were helping him improve his tennis talents. Rafa was hitting balls for an hour and a half every day, five days a week at this point. Toni would put in a lot of effort, encouraging him to constantly analyse his game. Rafa had won the Balearic Islands title in the Under-12s category by the age of eight. He was competing against youngsters aged nine, ten, and eleven in a competition open to children from all four islands of the archipelago: Mallorca, Menorca, Ibiza, and Formentera.

Toni refused to entertain his nephew. Even as his tennis prowess grew, he worked hard to keep him humble. He instilled in him the necessity of always respecting opponents and maintaining a calm, professional demeanour during matches. Toni acknowledges that he would downplay, if not dismiss, Rafa's accomplishments in those early tournaments. Rather than congratulating his nephew on his victories, it was his style to point out the flaws in his game. Any evidence of victory was swiftly thrown under the rug. Toni's stern techniques were regarded with scepticism by the other adults in Rafa's family. But, in the end, they all allowed him full reign to continue putting pressure.

Even though it was harsh, this strategy succeeded. Rafa went on to compete in the Spanish national championships at the Under-14 level in Madrid. During his first-round encounter, he collapsed, shattering the little finger on his dominant hand, the left. The agony was excruciating, but Rafa refused to give up. He didn't dare to complain to Toni, knowing he'd get no sympathy. He gritted his teeth through each match until he reached the final, where he defeated his close buddy Toméu Salva. When it came time for the winner's ceremony, the pain in his finger was so severe that he had to enlist the assistance of another player to hold the trophy up for the photos. Rafa was playing both tennis and football during this time in his life. In between, there was the extra stress of schoolwork. He was well aware that one of the two sports would have to be foregone. As much as he loved football and was a brilliant player, that was the one he chose to abandon. From then on, football was a sport he only watched or played casually, always rooting for his beloved Real Madrid CF.

Rafa would occasionally work with another tennis coach in Palma named Jofre Porta. Years later, Porta was still struck by the boy under his charge's determination. He remembered one particular instance when his determination shined brightly. Line judges are rarely used in junior tennis matches, thus players must call their own balls in or out. During a match, despite the fact that Rafa's shot obviously fell in, his opponent called it out. "He told me, 'It's incredible!'" 'He took the match from me!'" Porta recalls. "I sarcastically answered, 'I thought you were this fearless lad who could confront any problem?' He took a serious look at me, fought his way back into the match, and eventually won. This is a champion's mindset. I recall countless instances like this over the years."

During this time, the Nadal family owned two homes. In Manacor, there was a five-story apartment building near the city's beautiful church, Església de Nostra Senyora dels Dolors, with its towering, pointed spire and clock tower. Mother, father, uncles, aunts, cousins, and grandparents all spent a lot of time in one apartment building, all on different levels yet living in each other's pockets. They bought a second apartment building eight miles away, in the more beautiful seaside village of Porto Cristo, with the family split up across the floors. Rafa was a big fan of the setup. So much so that when he was 14, he was offered a scholarship to train at a tennis academy in Barcelona, on the Spanish mainland (called the High Performance Centre of Sant Cugat), his parents and Toni declined, fearing he would lack discipline living in a city like Barcelona without their supervision.

"This shows that if you have it in you, if you want to work, you can work anywhere," Toni subsequently said of the family's decision to keep him in Mallorca. "I don't want to believe that in order to be a good athlete, you have to go to America or other places." You can do it from the comfort of your own home. There have been two successful athletes in my family. Miguel spent his entire life at Manacor, and Rafa is doing the same to stay at this level. Rafa saw staying with his family as a significant advantage. It was a plus in terms of both serenity and organisation."

Nonetheless, a year later, they chose to send Rafa to the Centre de Tecnificació Esportiva Illes Balears, or CTEIB, in Mallorca's capital, Palma. He only came home on weekends. Tennis courts, an Olympic-sized swimming pool, an athletics track, a rugby pitch, basketball, volleyball, physiotherapy, and sports medicine were all provided by the taxpayer. But Rafa believes he was unhappy there. He was homesick, missing his family and his comfortable life in Manacor. He complained about his hectic schedule and struggled academically, despite passing his tests.

Porta, his high school coach, recalls it slightly differently. "Rafa was a typical student." His level of study was adequate, and he persisted until all of the travel made it impossible for him to study. Physical education was always his strongest topic." Rafa eventually persuaded his parents to remove him from school. For a time, he pursued a distance-learning course at the behest of his mother, who wanted her son to attend university. That didn't last long, as Rafa misplaced all of his school books while flying to the Canary Islands. "That was the end of my formal education," he said. His entire existence will revolve around one thing and one thing only from now on: tennis.

Rafa made his ATP tour debut in 2001, however his early appearances were at the lesser levels of ITF Futures and ATP Challenger tournaments. His first ATP ranking point came in September of that year, when he lost to fellow Spaniard Guillermo Platel in an ITF Futures tournament in Madrid.

In 2002, he made his ATP main circuit debut, competing in a clay-court tournament in Mallorca, which no longer exists. (A grass-court event named the Mallorca Championships is currently held in June, although it is significantly different.) In the first round, he defeated Ramon Delgado of Paraguay, his first ATP circuit victory. For the rest of the season, he won several Futures and Challengers, including minor titles at Alicante, Vigo, Barcelona, and Gran Canaria. It was all great preparation for his first big-boy bout in April 2003. With a world rating of 109, he was thrown in at the deep end when he made his debut at the Monte-Carlo Masters, an ATP Masters tournament at the level just below Grand Slams, at the age of 16. And what a start. He defeated Slovakian player Karol Kucera 6-1, 6-2 in the opening round. In the second round, he faced fellow Spaniard Albert Costa, the defending French Open champion and unquestionably one of the finest clay-courters on the planet at the time.

Rafa had a terrible year when he turned 18 in 2004. He had already participated in India, New Zealand, Australia - where he had reached the third round of the Australian Open, losing to Leyton Hewitt - the Czech Republic, Italy, Dubai, California, Florida, and Portugal by mid-April. All of this took its toll on his health, and by the time the clay-court season began, he was in excruciating pain, suffering from a stress fracture in his left ankle. Frustrated, he was forced to miss most of the tournaments on his favourite surface in spring and early summer, including Roland Garros. So, as soon as the fracture healed, he was eager to get back on the red stuff, and desperate to win his first ATP title.

He travelled to Poland in August to compete in the Idea Prokom Open, which was held at the Sopocki Klub Tenisowy, a clay-court facility overlooking the beaches along the Baltic coast north of Gdansk. The sixth seed was in good form after his forced break, having won every set he played that week. Furthermore, it was a great choice for a comeback tournament following his injury. It had failed to draw many dangerous players because it was held after the end of Europe's clay-court season, when the majority of the world's best were on the North American hard-court swing. Rafa was ranked 71st in the world, while all of his opponents in Sopot were ranked lower.

In the final, he faced another clay-court specialist, Argentinian player José Acasuso. The first set started slowly, with the most interesting point coming at two games all, 15-all, with Rafa serving. The rally was then played out over 19 shots. Rafa successfully had his opponent running up and down his baseline, from one side to the other, like a puppet on a string during this time. The latter returned everything thrown at him, but he couldn't control Rafa's movements in the same manner. Rafa easily won the final game, serving for the set at 5-3, due to some unforced errors from his opponent.

This was most people's first chance to witness the Mallorcan shine in an ATP final. He had reached and lost the final of the Auckland event in January, but that was on the other side of the world, in New Zealand. Rafa appeared to be in control again in the first game of the second set, with Acasuso serving, when he was abruptly granted three break points at 0-40. Initially clawing his way back to deuce, the Argentine eventually gifted Rafa the break of serve. The game proceeded with serve until 4-2, when Rafa broke again to go up 5-2. He was now serving his match penalty. While his court covering remained quick and ferocious, his serves were more cautious, no doubt because of the pressure of victory. Acasuso realised he needed to take risks if he wanted to win this match. He began hitting his groundstrokes flatter, blasting some rapid, accurate down-the-line shots that confused his opponent. He even used those shots to end the rally at the net. With each shot on the opening deuce, he pushed Rafa further and further back, until the Spaniard was virtually rebounding against the back netting. Acasuso finally broke serve. Was the Mallorcan going to squander it?

Rafa defended excellently the next game, returning shots that other players might have missed. At 30-all, he forced Acasuso to snag a return that went into the net for an unforced error by pushing him wide on his forehand. Rafa now has his first match point. The Spaniard chose to celebrate by leaping into the air and pumping his fists twice. He's unlikely to applaud an opponent's unforced blunder in that way these days. However, it demonstrated his determination to win his first ATP title. However, there was still work to be done. The first serve of Acasuso was dubbed a let. Under immense strain, the Argentinean couldn't believe the ball had clipped the net. He approached the chair and laid his palm on the umpire's knee, pleading for a re-evaluation. The latter smiled but was unmoved.

Perhaps he needed this distraction to break his opponent's concentration. The second serve was powerful, and Rafa was unable to return it. It took many more hard-fought points and a disagreement over a service call for Acasuso to hold serve and bring the score to 5-4, with Rafa still leading. The Mallorcan didn't want to drag things out any longer. He promptly finished the final game, bouncing up and down with his arms in the air as he won his first ATP title, 6-3, 6-4. "I was very calm out there today," he later said. "My goal at the start of the year was to be in the top 20, but I was injured for three months and am now aiming to be in the top 25 to 40 by the end of the year." The Sopot victory propelled him into the world's top 50, a position he held for the rest of the season, reaching the second round of both the US Open and the ATP Masters in Madrid.

CHAPTER 2

LEFT-HANDED

"For me, the Davis Cup victory over Andy Roddick, that's really the moment when Rafael Nadal became a champion, when he wrote the start of his story, when the public first started to know him."

Carlos Moya

Left-handed players include John McEnroe, Martina Navratilova, Jimmy Connors, Rod Laver, Goran Ivanisevic, Monica Seles, Thomas Muster, Jaroslav Drobny, Guillermo Vilas, Marcelo Rios, and, of course, Rafa Nadal. Lefty/righty pairings have also produced some of the greatest doubles teams in history, including the Bryan brothers, the Woodies (Mark Woodforde and Todd Woodbridge), Rod Laver and Roy Emerson, Tony Roche and John Newcombe, John McEnroe and Peter Fleming, and Martina Navratilova and Pam Shriver.

So, what is it about the left wing that attracts so many champions? Is there something about tennis that gives them an advantage? It turns out that there is, and it all comes down to the fact that left-handers are more rare. While lefties are used to playing against righties (since the majority of players are righties), righties are not as used to playing against lefties (because there are fewer lefties). Rafa (and his left-handed peers) have benefited greatly from this oddity throughout his career.

Chris McManus is a University College London professor of educational psychology and the author of Right Hand, Left Hand. "The left-hander is far more aware of their opponent's flaws than the right-hander, giving them a competitive advantage," he argues.

Norbert Hagemann, a sports scientist from Germany's University of Munster, conducted an unusual test on tennis players in 2009 to determine how they predicted shots from an opponent. He assembled a test sample of 54 right-handed and 54 left-handed players of varied ability levels, ranging from complete newbie to expert. He then had them watch video footage of expert right-handed and left-handed players before determining which way their shots would travel back over the net. His volunteers had a worse time predicting the stroke direction of left-handed players than right-handed players. Left-handers and right-handers both performed better in predicting the direction of right-handed strokes.

Hagemann emphasised a notion known as the strategic advantage hypothesis among academics. "Because players become accustomed to right-handed opponents' hitting patterns or playing style, attacks from the opposite side catch them off guard," he wrote. "Aside from the surprise effect, the motor responses to such an attack may be under-practised." Because left-handers attack infrequently, defensive reactions are less automatic and thus probably less effective."

It's a similar tale in other games where participants hit from one side of the body, facing their opponent, such as all racket sports, cricket, boxing, fencing, baseball, softball, and volleyball. Because lefties are more uncommon, they make for more difficult opponents. However, tennis does have one more aspect that benefits left-handed players, and it is all due to the geometry of the court. The majority of game points or break points in a tennis match come when the server is playing to the advantage side (the right-hand side as he faces the court). If the server is left-handed and the returner is right-handed, the former can serve wide to the right-hander's backhand side, which is usually the weaker side for most players. This means that when it comes down to it, lefties can employ their strongest weapon against their opponent's weaker arm. (Look at how Rafa has routinely pummelling Federer's backhand in this fashion, with devastating results.)

Right-handed servers facing left-handed returners, on the other hand, do not have the same advantage on crunch points because a wide serve would wind up on their opponent's forehand, which is typically their stronger stroke. (As a result, when Federer comes to serve, he is unable to return Rafa's slur across the net.)

Greg Rusedski, the British player who rose to fourth in the global rankings, put it succinctly in an interview with the BBC. "The left-handed serve naturally spins differently when you strike it, which makes it lethal coming from the left side of the court," he said. "Creating this type of spin - making the ball swerve and bounce - sends the ball far out wide, onto a righty's backhand." If my opponent can get the ball back, the court is open for me to take the point." It's likely that left-handed tennis players benefit from an extra X-factor. And it could be because their brains are wired differently than the majority of people's. In an interview with Sports Illustrated magazine, former American player Mary Carillo, a left-hander herself, discussed this. "Mainly, we're nuts," she explained. "You look at all the left-handers in tennis, and you've got some real wing nuts: Connors, McEnroe, Goran Ivanisevic, Guillermo Vilas."

She also included Rafa in this category of insane players. "That kid has a different spin on how to construct points; develop a rally," she continued. "He is creative and thinks outside the box." However, Rafa's left-handedness is a little more complicated than everyone else's. He employed a double-handed grip on both hands when he first started playing at the age of four, barely able to see over the net, to give him the force he required to send the ball back. Uncle Toni once told him that only a few professional players used two hands on both the forehand and backhand, and that he should switch to a single-handed forehand. Rafa did as he was told, preferring to use his left hand.

"I simply advised him to use his strongest hand," Toni explained once. "That's all there is to it."

Toni went into greater detail in an interview with Nike. "It's odd because the only thing he does with his left hand is play tennis." He always catches a ball with his right hand if he has to. He is a right-handed person. If he has to toss it, he always does so with his right hand. Because he lacked strength, he always played with two hands when he was little. I thought it was much better to play with one hand than two because there are very few professional players who play with two hands. Finally, we decided to experiment with the left. The first tournament he played with his left hand was challenging. But, well, it was a necessary step."

His mixed-handedness is complicated further by the relationship between his dominant hand and dominant eye. This is beautifully explained in the book Roger Federer & Rafael Nadal: The Lives and Careers of Two Tennis Legends by Argentine journalist Sebastian Fest. Fest talks about Rafa's versatility with Paul Dorochenko, an expert in the field, who explains how some players have their dominant eye and hand on the same side of their body (which is classified as homogeneous), while others have them on opposite sides of their body (which is classified as crossed). Rafa is crossed, according to Dorochenko, because his dominant hand is on the left and his dominant eye is on the right. "Crossed individuals tend to be poorly disciplined, inconsistent, and exhibitionist, but they are also more creative, intuitive, and better at making decisions," Dorochenko tells Fest, saying that 70% of top 100 world rankings players are crossed. "On the other hand, homogeneous players are hardworking, ordered, analytical, and cerebral, but pressure takes a greater toll on them and affects their decision-making negatively." Although it's difficult to accept Rafa's lack of control and consistency, you could probably argue his aggressive playing style stems from some form of exhibitionism. He's also creative, intuitive, and skilled at making decisions.

There's no denying that Rafa's switch from double-handed to left-handed was a stroke of luck. Just look at how right-handed opponents struggle to return his serve when it's fired to the advantage side of the court these days. Because of the slice, the ball swings extremely wide, driving the returner well beyond the tramlines. Even if the returner is able to scramble back a return, he is still completely out of position for the next shot. All of this raises an obvious issue. "Would Rafa still be as strong now if he used his right hand?" Toni once expressed his thoughts in an interview with Tennis magazine. "That's something we don't know and will never know."

There is one important match in every tennis player's career that marks the shift from junior to fully fledged adult. It was Rafa's victory over Andy Roddick in the second match of the 2004 Davis Cup Final between Spain and the United States. The Davis Cup Finals are the pinnacle of international men's team tennis, comparable to the World Cup in football. However, unlike the World Cup, the Davis Cup is held every year. Nowadays, the Davis Cup Finals feature 18 teams competing at three venues (typically in late November or early December), beginning with round-robin matches, followed by quarter-finals, semi-finals, and a final. Previously, the structure was different: 16 teams would play knock-out ties (best of five matches) throughout the season, ending with the strongest two teams hammering out the final, which was usually held in December. This final's five matches, played over a long weekend, including four singles matches and one doubles match.

In 2004, the United States and Spain proved to be the most powerful, with the latter entitled to determine the location of the final. Knowing that this would be one of the most popular sporting events of the year, but also that a clay surface would give them an advantage, the Spanish chose to hold the final at the Estadio Olimpico - or La Cartuja, as locals call it - in the southern city of Seville. It has a capacity of 60,000 seats and is used for football events, particularly those involving Spain's national team. It also has an athletics track surrounding the grass pitch. Because a tennis court would have taken up too much space in the centre, the organisers chose to situate the clay court at one end, with a temporary canopy erected above. Even when cut in half, there was room for 27,200 people, some of whom had camped out in the rain in the days leading up to the match to get the last tickets.

Nobody anticipated rooting for the squad's baby, 18-year-old Rafa. Originally, he was supposed to be one half of the doubles team. When paired with Tommy Robredo, the two would have been cannon fodder, forced to take on the Bryan brothers, the top doubles players on the planet at the time. Surprisingly, team commander Jordi Arrese decided Rafa to play in the second singles match, against USA's fearsome weapon, world number two and previous US Open winner Andy Roddick, at the last minute. No one was more surprised than Rafa. He saw himself as "the kid on the team," more of a cheerleader for his teammates than a real competitor on the court. He recalls being overjoyed at the idea of representing Spain. After all, this was the Davis Cup Final, the most prestigious team tournament in tennis.

But there was an issue. After Carlos Moya won the first singles match, the captain should have selected one of Rafa's far more experienced teammates - either Juan Carlos Ferrero or Tommy Robredo - to play the second singles match. Rafa was the lowest-ranked of the four teammates, having missed more than two months of the season due to a stress fracture in his left foot. He recalls seeing himself as the David to Roddick's Goliath. It was no surprise that he felt guilty, uncomfortable, and remorseful, especially because he had been promoted above his older and wiser colleagues.

Nonetheless, the urge to compete and the desire not to disappoint his comrades drove him to tackle his difficult assignment with unwavering, irresistible excitement. That early December Friday was cold and damp in a city where clay tennis is generally seen in the balmy spring or blazing summer heat. As a result, many people in the audience were wearing pullovers and overcoats. It was cold enough on the court at times that you could see the players' breath as they recovered between points. Both players immediately warmed up after being forced to thrash out lengthy rallies on the sluggish clay.

The opening set went to a tiebreak, which Rafa quickly won 5-2. Then anxiety set in. Roddick rallied to win the tiebreak and the set.

This is when the home advantage became clear. Rafa tore through the second set, winning 6-2, with constant encouragement from his fellow Spaniards. Although the American attempted valiantly to disrupt his opponent's rhythm by storming the net repeatedly, it proved to be a poor strategy. Even against Roddick, Rafa was often given the time he needed to cue up for passing shots on a surface as slow as that damp, winter clay. The third set was crucial in the match, as both players had set points. Roddick fought back two points on his serve at 5-6, while Rafa salvaged his one point in the tiebreak with a deft dropshot that his opponent ran for but couldn't put away. The Spaniard won the following two points, giving him the set.

The atmosphere in Seville that day was wild even by Davis Cup standards. With over 27,000 raucous spectators roaring every point Rafa won and every point Roddick lost (even unforced errors), this was the greatest crowd to ever see an official tennis match. (There were 3,000 more at the Houston Astrodome in 1973, when Billie Jean King defeated Bobby Riggs in the Battle of the Sexes, but it was an exhibition match.) Rafa later stated that he had done all possible to elicit energy from these blatantly partisan followers. Almost every winning point was punctuated by fist pumps, typically directed at his opponent. Those fist pumps were many at key periods, accompanied by leaps in the air, scissor kicks, and yells of ecstasy. Rafa later stated that he'd been silly to jump so high in joy, and that all that extra movement had caused more than a little cramping in his legs. Nonetheless, you could tell he was having a great time during this, his beautiful rite of passage.

By the fourth set, Roddick was wilting under the bombardment of both his opponent and the raucous audience. Rafa found himself serving for the match at 5-2 in the fourth set. He offered nothing fast or complex to Roddick's backhand. The match was then decided by a four-shot rally, which ended with Roddick hitting a frightened backhand long. Rafa slid backwards to lie down in joy, his arms and legs splayed out in a star pattern, his bandana falling to the clay. The fans roared with joy all around the court. "The noise in my ears felt like a jumbo jet flying low overhead," said Nadal later. "The audience was responsible for 50% of the victory." Rafa had fought for three hours and 45 minutes, his longest bout so far in his brief career. "There can be key matches in each period of my life," he explained. "This has certainly been the match of my life." Spain eventually won the match 3-2.

Christopher Clarey of the New York Times was among the journalists there that day. Rafa's performance was regarded as "transcendent" by him. "Seldom in the long history of the game have so many spectacular shots been hit from such extreme angles," he wrote. "And, while Roddick played beautifully and bravely at times, pushing forward much more than was predictable or prudent on such a slow surface and hitting some remarkable volleys," said Nadal, "his positive energy, passing shots, and baseline brio eventually wore him down."

CHAPTER 3

CLAY-COURT TENNIS

"The truth is that it [biting trophies] all started as a joke. But from then on there were always photographers who were asking me to do it. I kept doing it and now I have no option but to go on doing so because I can assure you that they don't taste good."

Rafa Nadal

"Clay teaches you how to suffer." So says famed Spanish coach José Higueras, who advised Jim Courier, Roger Federer, Pete Sampras, Sergi Bruguera, and Carlos Moya on how to excel on the red stuff during his career. He wasn't even exaggerating. Clay-court tennis has traditionally pushed players to their limits because of its longer rallies, broader angles, and increased physical demands. It's also a fantastic spectator sport. Especially if you appreciate watching two highly fit athletes waging attrition warfare from the baseline, grunting, running, and sliding through clouds of brick dust, waiting for the perfect opportunity to go in for the kill. Few players perform better in this regard than Rafa Nadal.

Clay-court tournaments on the ATP circuit are first held in February and March, during the South American summer, currently in Brazil, Argentina, and Chile. The focus then shifts to Europe, where hotel washing machines in some of the continent's most beautiful towns work overtime to remove the red brick dust from the players' gear. There are presently events at Marbella, Cagliari, Monte Carlo, Barcelona, Belgrade (twice), Munich, Estoril, Madrid, Rome, Geneva, Lyon, Parma, and Paris, the latter for the clay-court Grand Slam event Roland Garros. (There are other events in Marrakech, Morocco, and Houston, Texas, as well as five European tournaments following Roland Garros in Hamburg, Bastad, Umag, Gstaad, and Kitzbuhel.)

The fortunes and nationalities of the world's top players determine the fortunes and nationalities of the hosting clubs and localities, which is why, in 2021, Belgrade hosted two events (the Serbia Open and the Belgrade Open), capitalising on the renown of Serbia's most famous son, Novak Djokovic. There are four clay-court competitions, though, that glow the brightest and reddest of them, and these are the ones in which all players desire to excel.

The first is the Monte-Carlo Masters, which takes place in April in Monaco (well, actually just across the border in the French town of Roquebrune-Cap-Martin), and is widely regarded as the season opener, despite minor competitions the week before. The Monte-Carlo Country Club, with its steep hillside location and breathtaking vistas of the shimmering Mediterranean, provides a beautiful backdrop to some often beautiful tennis. If you become tired of watching the players, you may always turn your attention to the rich locals swanning around the club in their expensive attire, or the boats occasionally docked in the harbour. Monaco has been dubbed "the haves and have-yachts," and Rafa has won the title there 11 times, more than any other player.

The Madrid Open and the Rome Masters follow in May, each in their respective capital cities. The former is staged at La Caja Magica (The Magic Box), in the San Fermin quarter's Manzanares Park linear park. Rafa has won here five times, more than any other player. The Rome Masters takes place at Foro Italico, possibly the most distinctive location on the entire continent, with its iconic Italian fascist architecture from the Mussolini era. It harkens back to ancient Rome, with amphitheatre seating and massive classical statues, imbuing contests with a genuinely gladiatorial air. Rafa has won here ten times, which is more than any other player in history. But, in truth, Monte Carlo, Madrid, and Rome are only warm-ups for the big event, which takes place in Paris at the end of May with the clay season finale, Roland Garros (also known as the French Open). France's Grand Slam is outstanding in terms of grandeur and spectacle. The Stade Roland Garros, located on the western outskirts of Paris in the 16th arrondissement, is a 12.5-hectare complex with three stadium courts - Court Philippe Chatrier (15,000 capacity), Court Suzanne Lenglen (10,000 capacity), and Court Simonne Mathieu (5,000 capacity) - and 15 exterior courts.

Roland Garros, named for a legendary aviator from World War I whose buddy built the original stadium, has undergone significant renovation in recent years. A retractable roof over Court Suzanne Lenglen will be completed in time for the 2024 Olympic tennis event. The courts at Roland Garros are built with the engineering prowess of a major road construction. Deep layers of gravel, clinker, and broken white limestone extend far underground, all capped with a few millimetres of brick dust, which gives the courts their distinctive ochre tint.

"Of all the playing surfaces offered in this sport, clay is both the most physically demanding and the most technically subtle," according to the Roland Garros website. "It's a combination that, without a doubt, explains why, until the arrival of the king of clay, Rafa Nadal, Roland Garros was the toughest tournament for any player to dominate long-term."

And Rafa's dominance has been long-lasting. He has lifted the men's singles trophy, the Coupe des Mousquetaires (The Musketeers' Cup), 13 times, the first in 2005 and the most recent in 2020. Nobody comes close to matching this feat. It's quite improbable that anyone will. In actuality, the closest competitor is Frenchman Max Decugis, who has eight titles, but he completed prior to World War I, when the event was known as the French Championships and only members of French tennis clubs were permitted to compete. Bjorn

Borg of Sweden is the second greatest champion after Decugis, winning six singles titles in the 1970s and early 1980s.

Dicoculture Illustré de Roland Garros is a book written by Julien Pichené and Christophe Thoreau on Roland Garros. Here's what they have to say about Rafa's dominance: "Truly, this incredible hard worker, both a perfectionist and an insatiable player, appears to be the total, all-around champion." All of the most remarkable qualities of previous Roland Garros winners can be found within him: the consistency of Bjorn Borg, the scientific game of Ivan Lendl, the patience of Mats Wilander, the left arm of Guillermo Vilas, the bounding topspin of Sergi Bruguera, and the power of Jim Courier. In addition, he appears to have a Thomas Muster in each of his legs."

Despite the exaggeration, it's a genuine compliment. Consider Rafa's Roland Garros match record. He has competed in 108 bouts, only losing three of them. It's an absolutely remarkable accomplishment. The French Open is not the most well-known of tennis' four Grand Slam tournaments; that honour belongs to Wimbledon. It's also not the most entertaining - the noisy and raucous US Open in New York City wins hands down for sheer adrenaline. However, Roland Garros has a certain flair and panache that the other three do not. After all, it is Paris. When the world's greatest gather in Paris, there's always a distinct feeling of Gallic flare in the air. In normal years, this stadium complex represents the city of Paris enclosed inside a single tennis club. Inside the massive rectangular Stade Roland Garros, a network of tree-shaded promenades connects the numerous courts and decorative gardens. Because this is France, the meal is significantly superior to that of the other Grand Slams, as is the wine. And the audience is usually dressed more formally.

When the matches begin on the clay, though, all elegance is immediately abandoned. Clay court tennis needs the most physicality of any surface. The length of the rallies is what makes it so difficult. There will be none of the short, acute savagery seen on fast courts. On the red stuff, points can last 15 shots or more, during which combatants must progressively and tactically jockey themselves into a position from which they can execute a winner. "Playing on clay is like playing chess," concluded José Higueras. "You have more time to be creative and more options for what shots to take."

The top layer of red clay courts, ground into a fine powder, offers the ball greater grip as it lands, holding on to it longer than a grass or hard court would and slowing it down slightly. Because clay courts are softer than hard courts, the court absorbs more of the ball's energy. According to one study, tennis balls retain only 59% of their speed after bouncing on clay, compared to 60% on acrylic hard courts and 70% on grass. If there is moisture on the clay, which is common in Europe's northern cities, the balls will go even slower. Because of the greater grip, balls struck with high topspin have more kick after the bounce, frequently jumping up above an opponent's head. Rafa's groundstrokes are extremely efficient in this sense. Clay-court experts use clay-specific methods and tactics. The trajectory of the ball is an important aspect. Heavy topspin shots are used to take advantage of the increased spin that clay imparts on the ball. Slice shots are very useful, particularly on the backhand, since they keep the ball low to the ground, preventing opponents from approaching with their return stroke. Footwork on clay is virtually an art form, like a ballet. Many Mediterranean and South American players spend years practising their court slides. There are basically two kinds of slides. The first is when players sprint towards the ball, slide, balance, and then strike the ball. The second is when players hit their shot, when the ball is coming at them so fast that they have to strike it on the run, then slide in order to skid, change directions, and swiftly return to the recovery position.

It is critical to move tactically behind the baseline. If players like, they can typically stay close to the baseline during rallies on hard and grass courts. The added kick on the groundstrokes on clay requires them to sprint forwards to strike half-volley balls, or backwards to compensate for exceptionally high-bouncing balls. Dropshots are significantly more prevalent on clay courts than on other surfaces. It's not always because the bounce is lower. It's more that, with opponents frequently camped out deep behind their baselines, they have to run further to the net to get to a dropshot. How about physical fitness? Clay-court matches are typically much longer than grass- or hard-court matches, lasting up to three hours. As indicated by the number of players who experience cramps on this surface, the toll on the legs can be severe. A clay-court specialist's equipment differs slightly. The most significant aspect is racket stringing. Some professional players use rougher clay strings that grip the ball longer and allow them to add more topspin to the ball. Or they choose stronger, thicker-gauge strings, which allow them to impart more spin and force without launching the ball too far. Some even slightly lower their string tension to get extra force for those massive topspin shots. Hitting increased spin causes the strings to move significantly more within the stringbed, with brick dust particles lodged between the strings and creating abrasion. This invariably results in more string breaks. At the professional level, it's not uncommon for a player to break half a dozen or more strings in a single match.

On clay, players use special shoes with a herringbone pattern on the sole. This provides adequate grip, allows for sliding, and, most importantly, does not become clogged with clay. But there's always some leftover clay, so it's common for players to hit the soles of their shoes with their rackets to dislodge any particles inside the grips. And don't expect players to leave the court without some red paint on their clothes. If they take a tumble, they may wind themselves coated in it. Dirty clothes and shoes; lengthy, arduous marches; exhausted, cramping legs. Yes, clay is the most difficult surface for players. And those who can tolerate the most pain, like Rafa, wind up being the most successful of all. As Rafa famously stated, "I learned during my career to enjoy suffering."

"Rafael represents a new generation, a new wave." When the tournament director at the Monte-Carlo Masters discovered the 18-year-old Mallorcan had reached the final at the Monte-Carlo Country Club in 2005, he said wise words.

Everyone had praised Rafa's path to the final. He didn't drop a set in the first four rounds against Gael Monfils, Xavier Malisse, Olivier Rochus, and Gaston Gaudio. In the quarter-finals, he dominated Gaudio, the world number six and defending French Open winner, winning 6-3, 6-0. What kind of havoc may he cause in the final versus Guillermo Coria?

This skilled Argentinean, known as El Mago, or The Magician, had reached the French Open final the previous year and had reached world number three. However, ever since his ban in 2001 for testing positive for nandrolone (an infringement he blamed on a contaminated vitamin supplement), the clay-courter had been prone to anxiousness during crucial periods in matches.

Rafa blitzed through the opening two sets, upping the strain. "Once at an opponent's throat, Nadal is a fearsome sight," observed The Guardian newspaper's correspondent Stephen Bierley. His game is far from finished, but he has tremendous speed and a devastating forehand, as well as a lack of inhibition."

Nadal breezed through the opening two sets, 6-3, 6-1. But then, for some reason, his concentration wavered and the tide of the match shifted. He had lost the third set to love in less than a half hour. Coria must have believed he had a chance to turn the contest around. Rafa, on the other hand, proved he was made of tougher stuff. He quickly recovered and grabbed charge in the fourth set. He swiftly found himself 1-0 up with a breakpoint against Coria's serve, dressed in three-quarter-length Capri trousers, a white headband, and an orange sleeveless top that often masked him against the background of the court. Rafa would close in for the kill with brutal ease in instances like this, we all know. But, at the time, tennis fans - including, it appeared, Coria - had no idea what this young man was capable of. Rafa increased the strength of his groundstrokes and the volume of his grunting during the ten-shot rally. On shot six, he drove Coria back with a deep cross-court backhand, then a scorching forehand down the line, before finishing the point with the most delicate of dropshots.

At two games to love and 40-30 ahead, one of the most thrilling points of the tournament occurred. For 15 shots, the two players exchanged textbook baseline groundstrokes, each hoping the other would make a mistake. Then, on the 16th, Coria decided to throw in a surprise - and effective - dropshot that would have confused most players. Rafa, on the other hand, had anticipated it and rushed forward, blasting the forehand down the line. Coria easily intercepted the ball and returned it far into the far corner, as far away from Nadal as he could. Rafa then rushed back, just grabbing the ball to throw it back down the line to Coria, who was so tired by this point that he fluffed his final shot into the net.

Rafa eventually got his match-point opportunity. But it took another long rally - this time 16 shots - for him to win his first Masters Series tournament. He threw himself back into the court in joy. "This is incredible. Today I am extremely focused. "I'm very focused all the time," he stated after the game in his wonderfully shaky English. "Yeah, yeah, my first major tournament, no?" Everyone will remember this title. But my goal is to enhance my tennis. I need to work on my serve, volley, and slice. And if I do, if I develop these shots, do you think I'll be able to win a lot more matches?" It was a huge understatement. Rafa won three more Masters Series titles that year, as well as his maiden Grand Slam triumph at Roland Garros. By the end of the season, he had won a total of 12 ATP tournaments.

"I'm not superstitious; otherwise, I'd change the rituals after every defeat." I'm not even bound by routine. Because my head is generally incredibly untidy, what people term tics or routines are how I put my head in order. It's a technique for focusing and quieting the noises within. So I don't have to listen to the voice that tells me I'm going to lose, or, even more dangerously, the voice that tells me I'm going to win."

Rafa said this in a recent interview with the Italian newspaper Corriere dello Sport, explaining why he follows so many rigid rituals before and during his matches for the thousandth time. These rituals are a fascinating aspect of his personality, as they are many and, from the outside, serve no evident function. They have changed throughout time, depending on Rafa's mood, but they follow a general pattern.

Everything begins in the locker room. He reveals that 45 minutes before bouts, he must take a freezing-cold shower to stimulate his concentration and prepare his body for combat. Then he insists on gripping all six rackets he regularly uses on court. It has been said that he will not wear socks higher than 15 cm above his shoes, and that he will take his bandana out of his kitbag an hour before play, but will not wrap it around his head until minutes before he steps on court, always tying it gently, tightly, and perfectly. On court, he will frequently renew the bandana, tying it in the same concentrated, systematic manner. He'll perform intense hops and sprints while listening to music. Then he goes to the restroom. He has acknowledged taking five or six "nervous pees' ' in the final hour before the game.

Then comes a slew of pre-match rituals. Rafa insists on keeping one racket himself in large tournaments, where ball boys and girls carry players' kit bags onto court as a courtesy. He generally expects his backpack to be properly put next to his courtside chair whenever he arrives. (At one point, it had to be supported by a towel.) Now for the water bottles: always two, one cold and one room temperature, precisely lined up on the floor in front of his chair, to the left, with the labels facing diagonally towards the court. You'll notice that he always sips from each bottle at the end.

After the warm-up, Rafa tends to stay in his chair longer than his opponent, who is always the last man to sit. But then there's a sudden surge of activity as he sprints to the baseline before the start of hostilities. In between points, he modifies his gait to avoid stepping on the court lines. When the game is over, he always lets his opponent go past the netpost to his chair before passing it himself.

Before the serve, you should fix your sweatbands, headband, shirt, tuck your hair behind your ears, and bounce the ball a specific amount of times. After he approaches the baseline and receives tennis balls, a common sequence might be: Pull the left shoulder of his shirt up, the right shoulder of his shirt up, touch his nose, tuck hair behind each ear, and then begin bouncing the ball. His sponsors have spent millions designing some of the world's best tennis gear, so the shorts and shirt tugging have nothing to do with poor attire. It's just one of his soothing, centering exercises. He has stated that he is unaware that, in front of thousands of spectators and millions more on TV across the world, he strives to pull his underwear up through his shorts before every service; frequently a second time between first and second serve. "I've been doing that since I was a kid, so I can't change it," he told GQ magazine. "It's just something I won't be able to change." I can change a lot of things, but not this one."

It is true that illogical or superstitious routines and rituals can play a significant role in sports psychology, since success is based on believing. During his Wimbledon campaign in 2001, Croatian left-hander Goran Ivanisevic convinced himself that viewing the children's TV show Teletubbies every day would help him win. (Which he did.) When Serena Williams was knocked out in the third round of the French Open in 2008, she blamed her stunning exit on a failure to keep to customary routines. "I didn't tie my laces correctly, I didn't bounce the ball five times, and I didn't wear my shower sandals to the court," she explained. "I didn't have a spare dress." I had a feeling it was fate. That was never going to happen."

Other athletes can be even more perplexingly superstitious. Consider the English cricketer Mark Ramprakash. He attributed his strong batting streak in 2011 to chewing the same piece of chewing gum. If the game was over and he wasn't out, he'd stick the gum to the end of his bat handle "for when I resume my innings the next morning," he explained.

Mark Schwarzer, an Australian football goalkeeper, wore the same pair of shin pads throughout his professional career. First, at the age of 19, in 1990, and subsequently for every match until his retirement in 2016. "At various clubs, I had to tell the kit man, 'If you lose those, I'll kill you," he once explained.

Tiger Woods is famous for wearing a red shirt for the final round of his golf competitions, which he has done since he was a juvenile. "I just kept doing it because it was superstitious, and it worked." Nothing is going to change."

Is there, however, a method to all this superstitious madness? Back in the 1940s, one American psychologist proposed that we should learn from our feathery friends in order to comprehend human superstition. Burrhus Frederic Skinner, a behavioural psychologist at Indiana University (and later a professor of psychology at Harvard University), conducted a pigeon experiment in 1947. He put hungry birds in a cage hooked to a system that dispensed food automatically. Surprisingly, the pigeons immediately began connecting food with whatever random behaviours they were doing when it was presented to them, and they later believed that repeating these random actions would result in additional food.

Skinner published "Superstition in the Pigeon" in the Journal of Experimental Psychology. "Another repeatedly thrust its head into one of the cage's upper corners." A third developed a 'tossing' response, as if it were placing its head beneath an unseen bar and repeatedly lifting it. Two birds evolved a head and body pendulum motion in which the head stretched forward and swung from right to left with a rapid movement followed by a slightly slower return."

Rafa's water bottle placement, chilly showers, and underpant-pulling suddenly look less amusing. Skinner made the following comparison between pigeon and human superstitions: "The experiment could be described as a form of superstition in that the bird behaves as if there were a causal relationship between its behaviour and the presentation of food, despite the fact that such a relationship does not exist." Human behaviour contains several analogies. Rituals to improve one's luck with cards are good examples. A few unintentional linkages between a ritual and positive outcomes are sufficient to establish and maintain the behaviour in the face of numerous unreinforced instances. Another example is the bowler who has thrown a ball down the alley but continues to act as though he is controlling it by twisting and moving his arm and shoulder. These behaviours, of course, have no meaningful effect on one's luck or a ball halfway down an alley, just as the food would appear just as frequently if the pigeon did nothing - or, more precisely, did something different."

Rafa's rituals and routines, while having little practical effect on the outcome of a match, do serve to settle his mind. He believes they have an effect on him subconsciously. The power he has over these rituals compensates for the lack of control he has over other aspects of the match. "When I do these things, it means I am focused, it means I am competing," he previously explained. "It's something I don't need to do, but when I do it, it means I'm focused." Rafa has spoken about the necessity to become a "tennis machine" during matches, by suppressing his emotions, fighting back against his weaknesses, and therefore enhancing his chances of winning. This, he claims, is his interpretation of a mediaeval knight fighting in armour. "It's a kind of self-hypnosis, a deadly serious game you play to conceal your own weaknesses from yourself as well as from your rival," he reveals in his autobiography Rafa: My Story.

Then there's the tricky issue of his fears. He's admitted to having a few unreasonable concerns over the years. His mother has stated that he is afraid of the dark and likes to sleep with the lights turned on. She once told a story of her kid calling her in the middle of the night in a panic. "He called me and said, 'Mum, we've got a problem,'" she recalls. "'There's a power outage, and I'm terrified.' I had to tell him which drawer the torches' batteries were in." Rafa discussed his fear of the dark in an interview with Vogue magazine. "I'm a little nervous about being home alone at night." I had to sleep on the sofa at home. I can't bear the thought of going to bed. I'm there, with the TV and all the lights turned on. I'm not extremely brave in any aspect of my life. Yes, in tennis. In everything else, not so much."

Rafa used to hide beneath pillows during thunderstorms as a child. Even as an adult, he attempts to keep his family from going outside when thunder and lightning are predicted, according to his mother. Uncle Toni used to exploit his nephew's fear of storms to his advantage when he was young, in order to urge him to focus on the court. He warned Rafa that if he didn't concentrate 100 percent on his game, the thunder gods would become enraged. Every time, the ruse succeeded. The fear of thunderstorms, however, is only the top of the iceberg. Fast automobiles, motorcycles, helicopters, bicycles, deep water, house fires, dogs, spiders, and most animals... a whole slew of common situations make him nervous. It's reasonable that he's "terrified" of helicopters. However, if a professional needs to travel by helicopter, he will do so. He also tries to avoid motorcycles. "I have a motorcycle, but it was a gift, and I never use it," he once commented. "I'm not riding it." I'm afraid of motorcycles. That is extremely risky. "We only get one life."

Less reasonable is his phobia of driving, especially given that he has owned numerous extremely powerful sports vehicles. His mother emphasises how cautious her son is behind the wheel, frequently braking and accelerating and being wary of passing. Fear of the deep sea is unreasonable for an island lad as well. Rafa's sister once revealed that her brother wouldn't jet ski or swim in the ocean unless he could see the sea floor (something he must have accepted, given the paparazzi photos of him jet skiing with his wife and friends); and diving off high rocks, a popular stunt among Mallorca's children, is strictly forbidden. How about bicycles? He claims he was never comfortable riding a bicycle because he was always afraid of falling off.

Rafa's greatest worry, it appears, is that something awful will happen to his family. He is sent into a tailspin by the remote possibility of illness or accident. During the colder months, Rafa would repeatedly urge his mother to make sure the fire in the fireplace was completely extinguished before going to bed. If he was going out with his pals for the evening, he would occasionally call her three times to remind her. The intimacy of his relationships with his family cannot be overstated. This could explain why he has never left his island home. Many of his tennis peers have relocated to various tax havens across the world, but Rafa prefers to stay close to his family, despite Spain's top personal income tax rate of 47%.

Rafa's anxieties were heightened by the global Covid outbreak, as were those of practically everyone else. He was 33 years old when it happened, and he says he wasn't concerned about his own health. "However, if I get infected, I can infect people who are at risk," he explained in a recent interview. "I'm concerned about my parents, my family, and my community." It is the most difficult period of our lives. This is why we must fight for causes far more significant than a tennis match."

All of Rafa's rituals, routines, and anxieties combine for a riveting show on the court. Seeing that blend of perfectly trained athlete and terrified little boy is an intriguing glimpse into the man's character.

Carlos Moya, Rafa's coach, has compared his charge to Clark Kent's and Superman's two selves - the mild-mannered, bespectacled, socially uncomfortable nerd who, at the flick of a switch, metamorphoses into the fearless, athletic, triumphant superman. Rafa, like Superman, always exhibits characteristics of both his mild-mannered homeboy and his superman. As he has stated, "On the tennis courts, I may appear fearless on the outside, but on the inside, I'm terrified." "I believe that fear is a natural part of life." When Rafa won his first victory at Roland Garros at the age of 19, no one could have predicted he would go on to win 12 more titles on the Paris clay, more than any other player in history. In retrospect, we now recognize this great Spaniard as the unrivalled monarch of the red stuff, but 13 French Open wins were inconceivable at the time.

Rafa's level of play on clay courts increased tremendously over the late winter and spring of 2005. He won minor ATP tournaments in Brazil and Mexico in February. In early April, he reached the final of the Miami Masters on hard courts, losing in a thrilling five-setter against Roger Federer. Back on clay later that month, he won his first ATP Masters tournament in Monte Carlo, followed by championships in Barcelona and Rome. He looked unbeatable by the time he reached the final at Roland Garros, having defeated Richard Gasquet, Sebastien Grosjean, David Ferrer, and Roger Federer in preceding rounds. The vast majority of fans predicted him to win his match against Argentina's Mariano Puerta on Court Phillippe Chatrier. The King of Spain, Juan Carlos I, was among those who cheered. The fact that the monarch of Spain had travelled to Paris to observe the new prince of clay-court tennis demonstrated how highly regarded this young Mallorcan was.

Rafa began his maiden Grand Slam final with a bang, breaking serve in the opening game while wearing shoulder-length hair, his distinctive pirate-style trousers, a white headband, and a lime-green sleeveless blouse. Puerta then called a halt, walked slowly over to his chair, and asked the trainer to strap up his right thigh, with Rafa leading 3-1 and 40-15. If Rafa had any inkling that his maiden grand slam final would be done in under a half-hour, he was swiftly disabused as Puerta saved two game points and broke back to tie the game at 3-3. Despite his girth, the Argentinean showed no signs of weakness. Puerta consistently battered his opponent with poisonous shots that should have had him flailing as the two players continued to battle pugnacious groundstrokes. Rafa's defensive play, on the other hand, was outstanding, as was his ability to move swiftly into counter-attack mode. To the delight of the audience, nearly all of his winning points were accompanied with a fist pump and a loud yell of

"Vamos!" It's a celebration we've grown accustomed to, but in the early days of his career, his supreme confidence was startling. Puerta appeared to react to it with a mix of annoyance and amusement. However, he had called a timeout.

This first-set struggle quickly progressed to a tiebreak, with possibly the most pivotal point coming at 2-2, when an incredible 14-shot rally finished with Rafa pursuing a dropshot and Puerta guarding the net. Rafa then smacked his comeback directly towards his opponent's head, followed by another fist pump. To be fair, he did apologise momentarily thereafter, but the tension between the two players was now as high as it had ever been. Rafa then produced two incredible winners, a looping forehand into the corner and a backhand down the line that stunned everyone, including Rafa, who dropped his racket in awe. Puerta reacted to the Spaniard's dropshots and managed to pull himself into set-point position at 6-5. And then again at 7-6 before prevailing in the tiebreak to take the opening set.

Rafa's reaction was immediate and devastating. He was down a set for the first time in this competition. But giving up had never been his style, so he turned up the heat, chasing down balls that lesser players would have given up on. It all added up to some spectacular exchanges and a match that many consider to be a clay-court classic. Rafa broke Puerta's service again in the fourth game of the second set. After that, the Argentine, who had survived five-set bouts in the quarter-finals and semi-finals, began to lose his willpower. Rafa then dominated the third set as well, winning it owing to his opponent's double fault.

Puerta, on the other hand, discovered a source of energy. He had two set chances at 5-4 and 40-15 in the fourth set, but both were saved by acrobatic replies from the Spaniard. A third set point was also saved, thus instead of extending the match to a fifth set, Puerta was now facing break point himself. Rafa's lead has been reduced to 5-5. Puerta had blown his opportunity, falling 5-6 and 30-40 down when serving to stay in the match. He eventually crumbled, firing a forehand wide. Rafa collapsed, flat on his back, weary yet elated. The reign of the King of Clay had begun.

But there remained the King of Spain to attend to in the interim. Rafa climbed into the stands, his hair, shirt, and shorts smeared with brick dust, to embrace his parents, sister, uncles, aunts, support team, and close friends. Juan Carlos then leaned down from the president's box to congratulate his devoted subject, grabbing him by the sweaty biceps - the identical muscle that had caused so much injury to Puerta. Rafa, emotional and sorrowful, sat calmly in his courtside chair as the prize presentation was arranged. Finally, he made the lengthy trip to the podium, followed by one of the ball girls. The Cup des Mousquetaires was presented to him by great French footballer Zinedine Zidane.

Rafa and his crew celebrated their victory that night in a nightclub on the Champs Elysées. Meanwhile, congratulations were pouring in from all directions. Politicians in Spain were ready to get on the patriotic bandwagon. His official website was inundated with messages, including multiple marriage proposals. Years later, Rafa reflected with pleasure on his first Grand Slam victory. "I was rather young. "I had tremendous energy, youthful zeal," he recalled. "I was capable of returning difficult shots, winning crucial points, and doing so with strength and power." I played with genuine zeal. I had a good semi-final match, and the final was not an easy contest. But I felt fantastic physically. "I was confident in my game because I had won all of the previous tournaments [that spring], but I knew anything could happen."It all happened so fast. In two months, I went from being ranked 50th in the world to competing in the Roland Garros final. I handled it nicely and calmly. I had a good upbringing. I had planned for such an occurrence. After that triumph I came back to the hotel and I said: 'Okay, I won the most important thing that I can win in tennis. So for the rest of my career, I'm going to play with less pressure and more calm.' The truth is quite the opposite: you play under increasing strain each year."

CHAPTER 4

MAKING MONEY

*"Rafael has the one thing that Roger doesn't: balls. I don't even
think Rafael has two; I think he has three."*

Mats Wilander

Rafa's revenues from prize money and sponsorship are dwindling as
he nears the end of his career. He made a whopping $44.5 million in
2014, the year he won his eighth French Open at Roland Garros,
including $30 million from sponsors and $14.5 million from
tournament wins. By 2016, this had fallen somewhat to $37.5
million. It was back up to $41.4 million in 2018.

The actual amount that athletes make is an inexact science.
Accountants are unlikely to make their customers' tax returns public.
The American business magazine Forbes, on the other hand,
publishes its list of the world's 50 highest-paid athletes every year,
based on information from industry insiders on prize money, salary,
bonuses, sponsorship deals, appearance fees, licensing income, and
business endeavours. Conor McGregor, the Irish mixed martial arts
fighter, is at the top of the list, with total earnings of $180 million
from May 2020 to May 2021. Soccer legends Lionel Messi and
Cristiano Ronaldo are placed second and third, respectively, with
$130 million and $120 million. Roger Federer is the highest-paid
tennis player, earning $90 million. Rafa, on the other hand, is
nowhere to be found, having missed much of 2020 and 2021 due to
injuries or the global epidemic.

He's not about to tighten his belt anytime soon. During his long
career, he has accumulated roughly $127 million in match prize

money alone, making him the third-highest male player of all time, trailing only Djokovic ($153 million) and Federer ($131 million). This, however, pales in comparison to the massive sponsorship revenues he has gotten. Many different businesses have rushed to be connected with this player since he turned professional in 2001, with each new Grand Slam title he adds to his collection. His latest sponsors include his long-standing clothing brand Nike, racket brand Babolat, as well as Spanish financial giant Santander Group, car manufacturer Kia, Spanish insurance company Mapfre, Heliocare skin care products, Spanish telecoms company Telefonica, Swiss watch manufacturer Richard Mille, and Dutch beer Amstel (of course, the non-alcoholic version).

Rafa is far from the richest tennis player in the world. Roger Federer is the recipient of this honour. According to Forbes magazine, he earned $106.3 million in 2020, the most of any athlete on the planet. According to the newest rich list, the Swiss national is rated first among tennis players with $90 million, although in the ATP-logged calendar year of 2021, he only earned $647,655 of it in prize money. On the Forbes list, Roger was followed by Naomi Osaka, Serena Williams, and Novak Djokovic.

So, what is it about tennis that ensures such large sponsorship earnings for the top pros? It's largely due to television. During tennis events, the TV cameras focus on the players' faces and upper bodies in between points, ensuring that apparel brands are frequently shot. Matches can stretch three hours or more, especially on Rafa's preferred surface, clay, which adds up to a lot of on-screen time at the end of a tournament. Tennis is a global phenomenon (the men's ATP circuit holds events in over 30 countries across six continents), particularly among the rich middle classes, and receives extensive TV coverage from January to November. Sponsors see a good return on their investment.

However, Rafa, Federer, and Djokovic have an additional draw: charm, good looks, and enormous media appeal. Rafa has been winning Grand Slam titles since 2005, ensuring him global media coverage and, as a result, household-name status. While he does not speak a slew of languages like Federer, he does speak Mallorqui, Spanish, and English, the latter with some endearing peculiarities. His interviews are broadcast in many countries throughout the world in both Spanish and English. He's also attractive in a wholesome sort of way, and he's quite the clothes horse both on and off the court. He has previously modelled for Emporio Armani and Tommy Hilfiger, typically in his underwear.

Most of the brands associated with him, with the exception of underwear, are quite corporate in nature. This helps to explain why he is always so careful not to say anything contentious in interviews or on social media. With one slip of the tongue or thumb, he may lose a lucrative contract overnight. Many of Rafa's news appearances are little more than long-winded exercises in the fine art of saying very little at all. There have been a number of minor sponsors as well, although none of them are considered blue chip. He must have gotten a fantastic deal on his Sunreef catamaran, since he enthusiastically poses on the back for some of the company's promotional photographs.

While some of the larger brands require personal appearances, TV commercials, social media campaigns, shirt patches, and corporate handshakes as part of the contractual agreement, many of the smaller ones are content with a quick press conference, a couple of media appearances, and a brief mention on social media channels. His social media presence expands with each passing year. When this book was being written, he had 15.6 million Twitter followers, 14 million Facebook followers, and 12.2 million Instagram followers, with much of his output on these platforms devoted to advertising his sponsors. Rafa has even dabbled in the field of pop music. He appeared in the video for Colombian singer Shakira's song "Gypsy" in 2010. There was an English version as well as a Spanish one called "Gitana." Rafa's smouldering visage in the dry desert heat contributed significantly to the single's platinum status in Spain.

The video begins with the Colombian, Rafa's senior by nine years, playing a country music-style harp prelude while strolling towards the camera in a skimpy black halter top and skirt. Meanwhile, Rafa, all hot and sexy, waits anxiously in trousers and a white T-shirt, clutching to a chain-link fence, like a lovelorn teenager. Both Latin lovers are now lying on the ground, holding hands, snuggling, rubbing noses, and saying sweet nothings to each other. Rafa's shirt is suddenly off, and Shakira is straddling him, stroking his hair. The Colombian then hints at flamenco dancing, followed by more snuggling and a special dance for Rafa. Everything comes to a conclusion with a final kiss.

While the film undoubtedly improved Rafa's image, particularly in the Spanish-speaking world, it is by no means indicative of a potential career in acting. Furthermore, whenever he quits from professional tennis, the tennis player will have a plethora of commercial interests to keep him busy. He said as a young man that he had no desire to accumulate wealth. Rafael Nadal: Master on Clay, written by Jaume Pujol-Galceran and Manel Serras in 2008, detailed how he would delegate all financial choices to his father. "I have no idea how much money I make. That's not to say I don't joke about money, but I've never had to deal with it. I simply know that if I play well, I won't have any financial worries."

He said that the cheap cell phone he was using at the time demonstrated his apathy for money. "Of all the Spanish players, I have the most hideous phone." Because of this phone, people on the tour frequently make fun of me. All that matters to me is that it works. I don't need a cutting-edge device with a slew of features I'll never use. Some folks are content with having a Coca-Cola at the beach. That's my name. Others must drive a Ferrari or purchase a private jet. "To each his own." Needless to say, he now carries a far more expensive phone. Despite this, he still chooses to fly on regular airlines (in business or first class) rather than private aeroplanes.

Rafa and his family have amassed an enormous economic empire that now extends throughout Mallorca, Spain, and even internationally. His parents ran various local companies in Manacor and the surrounding area before he became a professional. His mother's family ran a furniture store in Manacor, a town where the industry had thrived for decades. Rafa's great-grandfather on his mother's side, a skillful cabinetmaker, was responsible for the family business's early success. Rafa's grandfather once informed him that in 1970, the Balearic Islands produced 2,000 wooden beds, half of which were produced in his own factories. That could be a stretch.

Rafa's mother, Ana Mara, later purchased and ran a perfume boutique, which she sold to focus on her position as a mother and homemaker.

Rafa's father, Sebastián, is now one of the island's most prominent and well-known businesspeople. According to his kid, dad is motivated by both money and the thrill of the transaction. He began working as a teenager, owning a tavern at the Porto Cristo beach resort. When he was 19, he sold used vehicles before briefly working in a bank. Then he moved into glass-making and glazing at a time when Mallorca's tourism business was thriving in the early 1980s, supported by a construction boom that demanded glass doors, windows, and tables. After a few years, Sebastián and his brother Toni acquired enough money to purchase the glassmaking company, now known as Vidres Mallorca, altogether. However, it was Sebastián who ran it, giving Toni time to coach his nephew.

Sebastián and Toni's economic empire grew from there, first focusing on real estate. Toni used to take half of the company's profits while doing almost none of the labour. The brothers were pleased with the scenario because Rafa's tennis tutoring was going so well. Rafa, his father, and his two uncles, Miguel Angel and Toni, formerly founded a property-focused company named Nadal Invest. Rafa's father also initially negotiated all of his sponsorship deals. Later, when Rafa began winning big sums of money on the ATP tour, as well as additional funds from sponsorship and commercial endorsements, his father suggested that the young player pay Uncle Toni a salary for teaching services. Toni instantly dismissed the proposal, fearing it would alter the balance of their relationship. He was glad to get money from his brother, but he didn't want his nephew to pay him because that would imply Rafa was his boss. Toni sought to establish himself as the boss of their tennis connection.

Rafa views his father as a hardworking businessman who overcomes obstacles and completes tasks. Rafa's approach to tennis matches reflects some of the no-nonsense industry. Sebastián now presides over a thriving economic empire that includes real estate, glass manufacturing, insurance, and restaurants. However, investments extend well beyond these industries and far beyond Mallorca. He is a director of Mabel Capital, a Madrid-based investment firm with over 300 employees operating in Spain, Portugal, the United Kingdom, and the United States. Rafa reportedly owns a 33% share in the company, which has operations in a wide range of industries, including finance, real estate, hotels, sports, media, and music. Madrid, Lisbon, the Costa del Sol, Philadelphia, and Los Angeles all have residential and commercial real estate operations. Earthbar is a brand of food supplements. There are two restaurant chains: Tatel, which has locations in Madrid, Ibiza, Miami, and Beverly Hills and is co-owned by Portuguese footballer (and former Real Madrid star) Cristiano Ronaldo and Spanish musician Enrique Iglesias, and Zela. Rafa became a significant shareholder in Real Madrid CF in 2010. His investment was viewed as a lifeline for the La Liga club, which was in debt at the time. His second uncle Miguel Angel, who is no stranger to the turbulent world of professional football, was employed as an assistant coach for a period.

Another notable economic venture for Rafa Nadal is the Rafa Nadal Academy. (Or, to be more precise, the Rafa Nadal Academy by Movistar.) Uncle Toni leads this massive sports enterprise in Manacor, with fellow Spanish tennis legends Carlos Moya and Carlos Costa serving as technical director and head of business, respectively. There are swimming pools, at least 26 tennis courts, football and squash fields, an international school, a museum, a health clinic, and a fitness facility. Rafa's business pursuits can occasionally overlap. The event took place at the Rafa Nadal Tennis Academy in Manacor, where he was presented with a brand new Kia EV6 electric vehicle. Tennis courts can also be found in Cancun, Mexico, and Sani, a village in northern Greece. There are courses for both amateurs and prospective professionals.

"Human training is equally important to us as sports coaching," explains Rafa of his coaching philosophy. "As a result, our goal is for each player to be capable of putting values such as hard work, humility, tolerance, patience, respect, discipline, and commitment into practice."

The Rafa Nadal Academy Kuwait is the most recent establishment to bear Rafa's name. The Sheikh Jaber Al-Abdullah Al-Jaber Al-Sabah International Tennis Complex has the first facility of its kind in the Middle East, with 15 tennis courts, two squash courts, a swimming pool, a 1500-square-metre gym, and a boxing ring. Tennis lessons, personal training, fitness classes, swimming lessons, and after-school programs, as well as a members' club, are provided.

The Nadals also make major charitable contributions through the Fundación Rafa Nadal (Rafa Nadal Foundation). Rafa and his mother created the foundation in 2008 to help disadvantaged children via sports and education, and it now has operations in Spain, India, and the United States. They say their mission is to assist kids "reach the full extent of their potential by empowering them and instilling values like self-improvement, respect, and effort." Rafa's mother serves as president, his father as vice president, and his wife serves as director. He is also aware of problems right on his doorstep in Mallorca. Rafa volunteered for hours to help clean up the area after heavy rain and flash flooding devastated the town of Llorenc des Cardassar in October 2018, killing 13 people and damaging hundreds of homes and businesses. He made rooms available for those in need at the Rafa Nadal Academy and contributed one million euros through his charity.

Much of Rafa's company is easily recognizable due to his unique emblem - two symmetrical bull horns and thunderbolts, a nod to his furious bull playing style.

Personal logos for the world's best tennis players are a relatively new phenomena. Federer's is likely the most recognizable - a modest monogram of his two letters, as quiet and polished as the player himself. It's particularly effective when seen on the blazer he frequently wears over his tennis gear when stepping confidently onto the court.

Djokovic's logo is a little more complicated. It's a mash-up of alpha (the first letter of the Greek alphabet), mediaeval Serbian initials, and a flying bird symbol that somehow merges to form his initials.

Meanwhile, Andy Murray's emblem combines his initials with the number 77, a nod to his management business and the fact that, in 2013, he became the first male British player in 77 years to win the Wimbledon singles title. Rafa's emblem is the only one that does not include his initials. It does, however, portray the dynamic and power that he brings to his game.

Rafa's fast increasing commercial empire, combined with his global sporting prowess, has caused the player himself to confess that his family has a certain Mafioso image - at least to outsiders. "There is something Sicilian about the closeness of the Nadal family circle," Rafa: My Story author John Carlin wrote. "They live on a Mediterranean island, and they are a clan more than a family - the Corleones or the Sopranos without the malice or the guns." They communicate in an island dialect; they are devoted to one another; and they handle all business within the family." Sebastián has frequently boasted that family devotion is significantly more essential to the Nadals than money. Maybe so. But that's easy to say when there's so much money floating about the clan.

All of this riches necessitates a significant tax payment. Rafa, unlike many of his tennis colleagues, has never been enticed to go to a tax haven. In this way, he truly is an outlier among his contemporaries. When this book was written, the majority of his peers in the top 25 of the ATP world rankings had relocated to countries with no or little income tax. Novak Djokovic, Daniil Medvedev, Stefanos Tsitsipas, Alexander Zverev, Matteo Berrettini, Hubert Hurkacz, Felix Auger-Aliassime, Jannik Sinner, and Grigor Dimitrov have all chosen Monaco, which has no income tax. Denis Shapovalov selected the Bahamas, Gael Monfils chose Switzerland, and Dan Evans chose Dubai to avoid their home countries' more harsh tax systems.

Rafa cheerfully pays the current top rate of personal income tax in Spain, which is 47 percent, but with somewhat clenched teeth. "I'm Spanish, and I'm happy to be," he recently told an Italian publication. "Of course, I'm less happy when the tax bill arrives." But I was fortunate to be born in a country of many qualities, which provided me with a pleasant life.``

In 2017, he went into greater detail about his tax situation. "In terms of asset management, it may be better to go to another country with better conditions, but Spain is where I'm happy, with my family and friends." In another country, I would have twice the money but only half the happiness. "Money cannot buy happiness." Rafa knows he would be unhappy if he moved away from Mallorca, his devoted family, and friends. Moving to a tax haven might save him millions in income taxes, but his mental health would suffer, and his tennis would suffer as a result. In the end, it would be a waste of money.

His scars from the previous year's Wimbledon final loss to Roger Federer were still deep. So, when Rafa returned to the All England Club in the summer of 2008, he was determined to leave as champion.

Despite having beaten Federer three times that year, all of his victories had come on clay. When it came to grass, the Swiss player's style of play gave him a unique advantage. But, in the run-up to the match, no one could predict who would win the psychological battle of minds that day. At this level of tennis, the mind is frequently the most powerful weapon.

Rafa's final hours of preparation for that fatal match were nothing out of the ordinary. He arrived at the All England Club at 10.30 a.m. on a dreary south London Sunday morning for a warm-up on the club's practice courts with his agent Carlos Costa, which was cut short by rain. After a basic lunch of pasta with olive oil and salt and a small piece of fish, he went to the locker room for a freezing-cold shower, which he claims energises him. He required a painkilling injection in his foot due to a previous injury. He sat in front of locker 101, wrapped fresh grips on his rackets, and then asked his physical therapist to strap up his hurting knees. Federer was also in the dressing room, a few paces away at locker 66.

Rain caused a little delay in the championship final, but both players made the lengthy, apprehensive walk down corridors and stairs to Centre Court, where they were greeted joyfully and excitedly by the maximum crowd.

Each player's demeanour and demeanour could not have been more dissimilar. Both were sponsored by Nike, but their uniforms were very different. Federer, ever the gentleman, chose a classic woollen cardigan with his renowned RF monogram imprinted on the left breast. Underneath was a similarly traditional polo shirt. Rafa was dressed in a zip-up tracksuit, a tight, sleeveless vest, and knee-length shorts. A big, white headband was something they both wore. While Federer's hair tumbled casually over the top of his headband, Rafa's longer locks were firmly held back.

Federer won the toss and chose to serve. The Swiss reigning champion hurled the first yellow Slazenger ball into the air and

47

smacked it hard at 2.35pm, 35 minutes after the official match start time. It clipped the net's top for a let serve. Federer's confidence stroke looked to be a winner when he returned the first serve, but Rafa just managed to return it. Then, unusually for the first point of a Grand Slam final, Rafa won a 14-stroke rally with a deep forehand to the far left-hand corner, beyond Federer's reach. It was only one of the 412 points that would follow, but it foreshadowed the epic encounter that was to come.

Many tennis experts consider what happened next to be not only the best Wimbledon final in the tournament's 144-year history, but also the greatest tennis match of all time.

It see-sawed back and forth, teasing the audience - and stretching the two opponents - again and again with suggestions as to who may win altogether.

Rafa subsequently revealed that he went into the match with a very simple strategy in mind: he wanted to "wear him down, break that easy rhythm of his, frustrate him, drive him close to despair."

It was a tactic that worked well for the first two sets at least. He won the first game 6-4 in 48 minutes and the second by the same score despite being four games to one down at one stage. A glacially slow service routine was one of the Mallorcan's techniques. Post-match analysis revealed that, because of all of his tricks and rituals, he took an average of 30 seconds to complete each service. Unfortunately for Federer, many of those serves in the second set went even longer. Pascal Maria, the umpire, eventually lost patience and imposed a time violation on Rafa.

The reigning champion needed some rhythm breaking of his own to turn things around. Rafa appeared to slide awkwardly on shifting direction in the third game of the third set. Fortunately, Michael

Novotny, the trainer, was able to rehabilitate his right knee and play resumed.

Rafa's routine was ultimately disrupted by the weather. With the score 5-4 to Federer, the rain began to fall and the players were escorted off the court. Federer attributed this rain break to a shift in pace, and the key to dislodging a certain lethargy that had crept in, in a documentary aired a decade later. "It took me two sets to shake it off, and I think the rain delay woke me up." "I told him, 'If you're going to leave this match, at least go out swinging.'"

When play began nearly an hour later, Federer had the upper hand as the competitors battled through to a tiebreak. With some blistering serves and forehands, the Swiss master won the tiebreak 7-5, and with it his first set of the match.

The next set followed a similar pattern, but the tiebreak was even more exciting this time. Federer had to preserve two championship points before rallying to tie the match at two sets apiece. Many have compared that fourth-set tiebreak to the greatest tiebreak of all time, Bjorn Borg's 1980 Wimbledon shootout against John McEnroe.

The rain again delayed proceedings at 7.53pm, with the fifth set tied at two games all, deuce. Many feared that the participants would have to wait until the next day to finish their battle. They resumed play, though, half an hour later, as the light faded.

The match's conclusion will be remembered for the rest of time. If the first rain delay aided Federer, the second was more advantageous to Rafa. He crucially broke the strong Swiss serve at seven games all. Half of the audience was chanting "Roger! Roger!" at the top of their lungs, while the other half was yelling "Rafa! Rafa!" In a final surge of vigour, the latter won the championship - on his fourth championship point of the match - by a score of nine games to seven.

As Rafa collapsed to the turf, landing flat on his back with his arms spread, the ball was still spinning around at the bottom of the net, where Federer had mistakenly played it low. He had finally defeated his Wimbledon adversary. Both players were physically and mentally tired after four hours and 48 minutes of the longest Wimbledon singles final in history. Many of the onlookers, who were cheering wildly, were also mentally drained. It was 9.16 p.m., and none of them had anticipated being on Centre Court at that hour.

Nadal made his way up to the players' box, where his family and friends awaited him. There were both parents, relatives, aunts, friends, professional golfer Gonzalo Fernandez-Castao, and the president of Real Madrid football club among them. He walked across the flat roof of the commentary booth, equipped with a Spanish flag, to the royal box, where his country's Crown Prince Felipe and Princess Letizia were waiting to congratulate him as well.

Rafa attempted to sum up his emotions at the post-match press conference following the trophy ceremony, which was performed in a dusk highlighted by the flashes of thousands of cameras and cell phones. "It's impossible to describe, isn't it?" I'm not sure. Just overjoyed. It's incredible to get a title here in Wimbledon. It's most likely, well, a dream. I used to fantasise about playing here as a kid. But to win is incredible, isn't it?"

The victorious Spaniard then dashed back to his rented house on Newstead Way, about a hundred yards west of the All England Club, to change into a dinner suit before making his way to the champions' party in town. He didn't get home until 4 a.m. the next morning. But when he slept, he slept like a first-time Wimbledon champion.

CHAPTER 5

RAGING BULL

"Some people get very confused about my game. They think it's better if the court is slow, because I have a good defence. But the faster it is, the better for me. My spin is more painful for my opponents, my aggressive game works better."

Rafa Nadal

Rafa has one of the most distinct, aggressive, and physically threatening playing styles among the top players currently competing on the ATP tour. Here, we dissect each component and examine what makes it so effective.

Forehand

Rafa's forehand grip is a semi-western grip, which means the face of the racket is slanted towards the ground when he brushes up through the ball. The racket head begins in front of him, glides past the left side of his face, and then swings far behind him, low to the ground. He uses his entire body like a huge whip to impart such strong topspin, uncoiling each section - leg, buttocks, belly, shoulder, arm, and wrist - in succession to increase the revolutions per minute (RPM) on the ball. The racket head moves across the front of his body, strikes the ball (with his entire torso open at this point), and then moves all the way around the back of his body, finishing at his left shoulder.

The lasso, or buggy whip, is a more infamous form of his forehand, with a genuinely devastating amount of topspin. It was dubbed "the Nadalada" by Rafa and his trainers. The preparation is the same as described previously, but the racket follow-through is significantly higher. In reality, after striking the ball, the racket swings upwards, over and around his head, grazing the top of his cranium and concluding with the racket head pointing exactly behind him. It's an incredible image to witness, almost as if he's holding a lasso rope, twisting his rotator cuff and elbow beyond what you'd believe was physically possible.

The exact number of RPM he imparts on the tennis ball changes dramatically with each shot. Some estimate it to be well over 3,000 RPM, while others believe it to be considerably higher. It depends on the weather, the court surface (he smashes forehands flatter when he isn't on clay, for example), how deep he wants to send the ball, and how much time he has to prepare for the shot.

This forehand has been thoroughly examined by one tennis teacher. John Yandell of San Francisco employed a high-speed camera to count the average number of spins on a tennis ball damaged by Rafa's lasso forehand. "We measured one forehand Nadal hit at 4,900 RPMs," he told the New York Times. "His average RPM was 3,200. Consider that for a moment. It's a little unsettling to think about. A ball travels between the players' rackets in around a second. So, in the second it took to reach [his opponent's] racket, a Nadal forehand would have rolled over 80 times."

Rafa's ability to weaponize his forehand is astounding, especially on clay. Because of the strong topspin, he can smash the ball harder, causing it to travel faster but still loop down inside the baseline. When the ball lands on the court, the topspin causes it to kick up swiftly and suddenly. If opponents do not immediately attack, the ball will bounce high above their heads. This means they have very little time to plan or execute their follow-up shots.

"I try to put the ball deep, and then it bounces up really high," Rafa says. It compels my opponent to enter the court, but at great risk.

Alternatively, he must hit it three metres behind the baseline. So it's either defence or a dangerous attack."

Rafa's hitting partner famously described returning this forehand as "breaking off your arm." In an interview with the New York Times, American coach Robert Lansdorp highlighted Rafa's lasso forehand's effectiveness: "He can do it from anywhere, almost to any ball, and make winners." He can hit it cross-court, down the line, or anywhere he wants. And he's probably been doing it since he was ten. Thank goodness no one modified it and told him, 'Hey, that's not how you hit a forehand.'"

Backhand

Rafa's ability to weaponize his forehand is astounding, especially on clay. Because of the strong topspin, he can smash the ball harder, causing it to travel faster but still loop down inside the baseline. When the ball lands on the court, the topspin causes it to kick up swiftly and suddenly. If opponents do not immediately attack, the ball will bounce high above their heads. This means they have very little time to plan or execute their follow-up shots.

"I try to put the ball deep, and then it bounces up really high," Rafa says. It compels my opponent to enter the court, but at great risk. Alternatively, he must hit it three metres behind the baseline. So it's either defence or a dangerous attack."

Rafa's hitting partner famously described returning this forehand as "breaking off your arm." In an interview with the New York Times, American coach Robert Lansdorp highlighted Rafa's lasso forehand's effectiveness: "He can do it from anywhere, almost to any ball, and make winners." He can hit it cross-court, down the line, or anywhere he wants. And he's probably been doing it since he was ten. Thank goodness no one modified it and told him, 'Hey, that's not how you hit a forehand.'"

Serve

Rafa's serve was once his weakest weapon, frequently slow in comparison to his opponents. He acknowledged it. It's not unexpected given how he had to deal with his multi-handedness. However, as his career developed, it became more of a weapon, with aces and service winners becoming increasingly common. His initial serve - usually sliced, especially from the left side, but sometimes flatter - now regularly exceeds 120mph. Throughout his ATP circuit career, he has hit over 3,780 aces, including about 2,220 on hard courts, 950 on clay, and 600 on grass.

His second serve is slower and safer, either topspin or slice. According to an ATP research from 2019, it averaged 96.4mph, barely ahead of Djokovic and Federer. In the same study, Rafa's second serve had a greater victory % than any other player in that year's world top ten - again, slightly ahead of Djokovic and Federer.

Rafa's serve, as a left-hander, is especially successful when played to a right-hander in the advantage court (as he sees it) because it swings out wide, far beyond the tramlines, dragging the opponent out of position. If he applies significant topspin to it, it will kick up high, making it even more difficult for a right-hander to return. Federer has struggled with this component of Rafa's serve for many years.

Rafa employs a stance dubbed the pinpoint stance to prepare for his serve, in which his back foot gets closer to his front foot as he takes the racket back behind his back. Alex Corretja, a former Roland Garros finalist, recently examined Rafa's serve, describing how it differs from the one he used earlier in his career. Rafa, for example, does not bend his knees as much as he did when starting the service movement, instead adopting a more erect stance. This allows him to rapidly return to the ready position after the serve in preparation for the next shot. He also raises the racket on his serve, opening up his wrist when striking the ball and increasing the speed of his serves.

Craig O'Shannessy of the ATP tour has thoroughly examined Rafa's serve. Here are some of his 2019 season findings: Most first serves (62%) are sliced down the T at the start of the service game, while 25% are served wide and only 13% are sent to the opponent's body. "The thinking here is to start the game on the right foot with what he knows best, and surge to 15-love as many times as possible," O'Shannessy explains. At 15-all, 51% of first serves are down the T, 36% are wide, and 13% are at the body. If he is 30-love up, he gives himself some breathing room and can afford to be a little more creative, sending the majority of his serves (52%) out wide, 42% down the T, and only 6% to his opponent's body. If he's 30-love down, he'll have to be more careful, sending 49% wide, 37% down the T, and 15% to the body.

Physical and mental game

Rafa wins by wearing down his opponents and waiting for the right opportunity to kill the point. "My game is to play with the rallies," he once said. "I don't want to play serve-and-volley, serve and one shot, or serve and ace." Everyone must be aware of this. My game consists of playing with energy, maintaining a consistent rhythm, and attempting to play for an extended period of time without making mistakes."

He needs amazing footwork and clever court coverage to make this attritional kind of tennis work, which he has transformed into an art form that is frequently mesmerising to watch.

However, physical strength is meaningless without mental fortitude. Djokovic has been quite complimentary of his opponent's combination. "Rafael is the physically strongest player on the tour," he stated once, "and mentally he has this unbelievable ability to stay focused from the first to the last point of the match, whether he's playing in the Wimbledon final or the first round of a minor tournament."

Guy Forget, a former French Davis Cup captain, said it even better. "Nadal is a brutal force." He has the mental fortitude to face everything. Even when he's in difficulties, even when his feet are blistered, he manages to dominate. He's a defensive beast. You believe you've won the point when he's back in the sponsor's hoarding, five metres behind the baseline, and then he pulls off a passing shot that everyone marvels at."

The grunting

Rafa is far from the only player to grunt loudly upon striking the ball. He will not be the last. Many players have filled tennis arenas with the sound of loud grunting or shrieking, from Jimmy Connors in the 1970s to Monica Seles in the 1990s and, more recently, the Williams sisters, Maria Sharapova, Victoria Azarenka (or 'Vika the shrieker,' Andy Murray, and Novak Djokovic. Rafa's are quieter than those of many other players.

He'd be wise not to break the habit. According to experts, grunting while striking the ball provides a modest percentage of extra force to each shot. It gives players more confidence on the court. According to renowned American coach Nick Bollettieri, grunting provides players with a "psychological and physiological release of tension." There are further advantages. When one player hits the ball, the opponent uses the sound of the ball on the racket to determine the speed and depth of the stroke coming towards him. Grunting masks this sound, putting the opponent at a little disadvantage.

Rafa's racket

Rafa has been playing tennis with Babolat rackets since he was eight years old. He has fine-tuned the numerous models over the years. He favoured the lighter Soft Drive type as a child, subsequently progressing to the Pure Drive. In 2004, he began using the new Aero model. "It was engineered specifically for spin," according to the company. "With an aerodynamic section to increase head speed, giving the ball more rotations per minute, it proved ideal for Nadal's topspin-heavy game that was about to conquer the tennis world."

The racket strings are very important in Rafa's topspin game. Although he has used Luxilon Big Banger strings at times over his career, he began using an octagonal (rather than the more common cylindrical) string called the Babolat RPM Blast in late 2009. "Sheathed in silicon, it grabs the ball for better lift and spin," the producers say. "Everyone held their breath when Rafa agreed to try the RPM Blast. After about 15 minutes, he declared the verdict: 'not bad'. Just a few days later, his coach Toni Nadal left a message for the competition department, saying, 'The string is really nice indeed. We require more!"

In 2011, he asked Babolat to add extra weight to the top of the racket head to create greater head speed on his shots as he began positioning himself further up the court for his groundstrokes - closer to the baseline than he used to play. "Babolat's customisation team worked on the addition of a sliver of weight tape at the top of his frame to increase the powerful hammer effect," the company says. "That added three grams to the weight, which is a significant increase in relative terms." In 2016, two grams of tape were added to the frame's top.

The Babolat Pure Aero RAFA is the most recent edition of Rafa's Aero. Guillaume Cambon is one of the technicians who works on the frame for Babolat. "Aside from these strips of weight tape at the top of the frame, his racket has almost no specific customization," he claims. Jean-Christophe Verborg is the director of competition at Babolat. He claims that his client receives a batch of six to eight new rackets four times a year. It is crucial to note that almost no higher-ranked professional players utilise the same model of racket as is available to the general public. Almost all of them personalise them in some way. No serious elite player would consider purchasing a new racket online or from a sports goods store and immediately stepping onto the court with it. Every facet, just like racing automobiles, must be perfected. Some players have even been known to utilise a different brand of racket underneath the paint job of their sponsor. (There is no indication that Rafa does this.)

The strings are the first to get notice. Rackets are sold unstrung in almost every country across the world (excluding the UK, for some strange reason) so that players can choose their own stringing set-up. This is a highly intricate business among the top pros, needing experienced racket stringers who thread their players' rackets with strings of a specified substance, gauge, pattern, and tension.

Most players also use strips of lead to alter the weight, balance and head speed of their rackets, sticking it to the frame, like Rafa. Some even open up the butt cap at the base of the racket handle and insert extra weight inside in the form of lead, silicone or epoxy.

The handle itself is often different to the handle you'll see on rackets in the shops. Many pros are so meticulous in their demands that they ask their racket technicians to change the ratio of the bevels on the handle, for example, or even the length of the handle in some cases.

So what exactly is the weapon that Rafa goes into battle with? It depends who you believe. Babolat insists he uses the Babolat Pure Aero RAFA. But most experts suggest he actually plays with a heavier and less forgiving model called the Babolat AeroPro Drive Original.

Rafa's grip size selection is relatively small, especially given that he does not have small hands. However, the player argues that this lets him generate more topspin. "I like the small grip because it gives me more control over what I'm doing with my hand," he told GQ magazine. "With a larger grip on my hand, I can produce more spins."

Rafa's current Babolat RPM Blast strings, according to Hudson, have a 15L gauge/1.35mm and are strung at a tension of 55 pounds per square inch. "At the start of 2016, Nadal briefly switched to Luxilon Big Banger Original 130 strings to obtain more power," he continues. "While the string did provide more power, Nadal felt he had less control due to the strings moving more (becoming more spaced out), and he quickly returned to the Babolat RPM Blast setup."

Surprisingly, Rafa never throws or smashes his racket in exasperation. "Because I was taught as a child that it is not done," he once explained. "I am at fault, not the racket."

Rafael Nadal's self-discipline has been examined by Jaume Pujol-Galceran and Manel Serras, the Spanish writers of Rafael Nadal: Master on Clay. "Nadal has never smashed his racket on the ground in anger," they claim. "He never says anything out of place, and he never makes a careless gesture towards his opponents." On the court, he is always respectful. He does jump, gesticulate, and brandish his fist a few times, but never to taunt the opposing player, only to connect with his family and friends. Toni trained him to politely thank his opponent after every match, regardless of the outcome. He never lost his sense of appropriateness while on tour."

Rafa's grip size selection is somewhat limited, especially given that he does not have small hands. However, the player argues that this enables him to generate more topspin. "I like the small grip because it gives me more control over what I'm doing with my hand," he stated in an interview with GQ magazine. "I can produce more spins than when I have a tighter grip on my hand."

Rafa's current strings, according to Hudson, have a 15L gauge/1.35mm and are strung at a tension of 55 pounds per square inch. "At the start of 2016, Nadal briefly switched to Luxilon Big Banger Original 130 strings to obtain more power," he adds. "While the string did provide more power, Nadal felt he had less control due to the strings moving more (becoming more spaced out), and it didn't take long for him to return to the Babolat RPM Blast setup."

Surprisingly, you'll never see Rafa toss or break his racket in frustration. "Because as a child, I was taught that it is not done," he once explained. "I, not the racket, am at fault."

Rafael Nadal's self-discipline has been studied by Jaume Pujol-Galceran and Manel Serras, the Spanish authors of Rafael Nadal: Master on Clay. "Nadal has never smashed his racket on the ground in anger," they write. "He never says anything out of place, and he never makes a rash gesture towards his opponents." On the court, he always displays respect. He does leap, gesticulate, and raise his hand a few times, but never to taunt the opposing player, merely to connect with his family and friends. Toni taught him to courteously applaud his opponent after every match, regardless of the outcome. It was an accuracy he never lost while on tour."

"In February 2017, I was in Budapest, interviewing a South Korean tennis player," Cazzaniga recalls. "It just so happened that Toni Nadal was also in Budapest for a tennis coaches' conference, so I took advantage of the opportunity to interview him as well."

Toni dropped a bombshell during their talk at one point. He told Cazzaniga that he would stop tutoring Rafa and start working at the Nadal Tennis Academy the following year.

"'Wait!' I said. 'Did you realise we're taping this conversation?'" Cazzaniga recalls. "'Yes, I know,' Toni said, as if breaking up with his nephew after 27 years was the most ordinary thing in the world." I asked him three times if he wanted everyone to know, and he confirmed that he did."

Cazzaniga, understandably, felt Rafa was already aware of Toni's choice, so he immediately publicised the news on his website TennisItaliano.it. Toni's statements from that interview have been translated:

"Rafa and I never had a disagreement." But until he was 17, I made all of the decisions. Then came the agent Carlos Costa, his father grew closer to him, and everyone had an opinion. And the truth is that with each passing year, I get to decide less and less, until I won't be able to decide anything at all."

The tale was all over the world in the press the next day. The New York Times, El Pais, L'Equipe, and other major newspapers and websites around the world published notable articles. Rafa, on the other hand, had no idea his uncle was preparing to end the relationship. Cazzaniga was shocked to receive a phone call from Rafa's communications chief requesting to hear the original recording of the interview with Toni. Cazzaniga claimed that he assumed Rafa and Toni had already agreed to split, and that he had no intention of releasing such a shock.

Cazzaniga is still perplexed as to why Toni chose to inform him of the news before informing his nephew. "Perhaps he thought Rafa wanted to split up the coaching partnership but couldn't fire his uncle." He had been with him since he was four years old, after all. Toni may have made the decision to keep his nephew from having to make the decision himself. In essence, I believe he split so Rafa wouldn't have to." With Toni out of the picture, Carlos Moya is now Rafa's primary coach. He was a highly talented player himself in the 1990s and 2000s and has practised with him since turning pro. He won the French Open in 1998 and rose to world number one the following year. In addition to Roland Garros, he won 19 singles titles on the ATP tour, including three Masters Series.

Francis Roig is Rafa's assistant coach, a position he held for many years under Toni. During the 1980s and 1990s, Roig was a useful player, reaching a career high of number 23 in doubles and number 60 in singles. Carlos Costa was Rafa's agent for many years during the Toni dictatorship, working through the all-powerful worldwide sports and entertainment agency IMG. Costa now represents Rafa as an independent agent, likely saving the Nadal family a small fortune in agency fees.

His doctor Angel Ruiz Cotorro (who has been treating him since he was 14 years old) and his communications chief Benito Pérez Barbadillo ("irreverent, quick-witted, always cracking jokes") are two additional key members of the Toni support team who have remained. There's also physical trainer Joan Forcades, though Rafa uses his services less and less as his career winds down.

Rafa's support team

For 27 years, they were one of tennis' most famous pair acts. Uncle Toni and Rafa. What would one be without the other, living in and out of each other's pockets?

Their relationship, however, gradually became a love-hate affair. Rafa had a profound respect for his uncle that bordered on devotion. As a child, he imagined Toni had supernatural abilities. Toni told Rafa that he had won the Tour de France, played centre forward for AC Milan, and had the miraculous ability to make it rain whenever he wanted. Rafa dubbed his uncle "Mago" (Magician).

At the same time, Rafa frequently described his uncle as "grumpy" and "quarrelsome." Toni's coaching methods bordered on the brutal. For instance, uncle and nephew would compete in matches in which the winner was the first to score 20 points. Toni would let Rafa get to 19 points before accelerating and slamming him off the court, 20 points to 19.

Toni, who used to play national rather than international level tennis, had strong beliefs about how children should be raised, refusing to indulge them in any way.

Toni stepped down as Rafa's coach in 2017. The narrative of how these two ostensibly inseparable people finally split ways is strange. Toni was with Italian journalist Lorenzo Cazzaniga when the coach abruptly declared his decision to stop working with his nephew.

"In February 2017, I was in Budapest, interviewing a South Korean tennis player," Cazzaniga recalls. "It just so happened that Toni Nadal was also in Budapest for a tennis coaches' conference, so I took advantage of the opportunity to interview him as well."

Toni dropped a bombshell during their talk at one point. He told Cazzaniga that he would stop tutoring Rafa and start working at the Nadal Tennis Academy the following year.

"'Wait!' I said. 'Did you realise we're taping this conversation?'" Cazzaniga recalls. "'Yes, I know,' Toni said, as if breaking up with his nephew after 27 years was the most ordinary thing in the world." I asked him three times if he wanted everyone to know, and he confirmed that he did."

Cazzaniga, understandably, felt Rafa was already aware of Toni's choice, so he immediately publicised the news on his website TennisItaliano.it. Toni's statements from that interview have been translated:

"Rafa and I never had a disagreement." But until he was 17, I made all of the decisions. Then came the agent Carlos Costa, his father grew closer to him, and everyone had an opinion. And the truth is that with each passing year, I get to decide less and less, until I won't be able to decide anything at all."

The tale was all over the world in the press the next day. The New York Times, El Pais, L'Equipe, and other major newspapers and websites around the world published notable articles.

Rafa, on the other hand, had no idea his uncle was preparing to end the relationship. Cazzaniga was shocked to receive a phone call from Rafa's communications chief requesting to hear the original recording of the interview with Toni. Cazzaniga claimed that he assumed Rafa and Toni had already agreed to split, and that he had no intention of releasing such a shock.

Cazzaniga is still perplexed as to why Toni chose to inform him of the news before informing his nephew. "Perhaps he thought Rafa wanted to split up the coaching partnership but couldn't fire his uncle." He had been with him since he was four years old, after all. Toni may have made the decision to keep his nephew from having to make the decision himself. In essence, I believe he split so Rafa wouldn't have to."

With Toni out of the picture, Carlos Moya is now Rafa's primary coach. He was a highly talented player himself in the 1990s and 2000s and has practised with him since turning pro. He won the French Open in 1998 and rose to world number one the following year. In addition to Roland Garros, he won 19 singles titles on the ATP tour, including three Masters Series.

Francis Roig is Rafa's assistant coach, a position he held for many years under Toni. During the 1980s and 1990s, Roig was a useful player, reaching a career high of number 23 in doubles and number 60 in singles. Carlos Costa was Rafa's agent for many years during the Toni dictatorship, working through the all-powerful worldwide sports and entertainment agency IMG. Costa now represents Rafa as an independent agent, likely saving the Nadal family a small fortune in agency fees. His doctor Angel Ruiz Cotorro (who has been treating him since he was 14 years old) and his communications chief Benito Pérez Barbadillo ("irreverent, quick-witted, always cracking jokes") are two additional key members of the Toni support team who have remained. There's also physical trainer Joan Forcades, though Rafa uses his services less and less as his career winds down.

Rafa's physical therapist Rafael Maymó, or Titan, as he's known, is a member of the squad who is possibly more vital than all of the others combined. Maymó is in charge of more than simply Rafa's physical appearance. He's a valuable blend of physio, shrink, confidant, man Friday, and shoulder to weep on. Rafa's playing technique and tactics do not demand the most attention as he nears the end of his career. It is about his physical and emotional health. Maymó takes excellent care of both.

"He is so important for Rafa's career," Cazzaniga said about Titan. He is one of his closest friends and the only one who has been by his side throughout his career and at all events. Sometimes Toni couldn't make it to a competition, and sometimes Carlos Moya couldn't either. However, Maymó is always present. He understands Rafa better than anybody else. Even more so than Toni. When Rafa had a personal problem, he went to Maymó rather than Toni. Even when Rafa's father needed to ask about Rafa, he turned to Maymó rather than Toni. Maymó is more knowledgeable about Rafa than even his wife.``

Rafa confirmed the two's intimate relationship. "Without Tint on my team, I'd be alone," he noted in his autobiography Rafa: My Story. "If he left, it would be nearly impossible to fill the void of friendship he'd leave behind." He is not just a wonderful person, but he is also dependably honest. If he has something to say to you, he will say it straight.``

Rafa's fitness regime

Rafa's training practices on and off the court are jealously guarded secrets. According to the Wall Street Journal, "Team Nadal sees no benefit in disclosing confidential information that could be useful to his rivals." However, it is apparent that Rafa has worked hard over the years to bulk up his muscles in order to compete so aggressively on the court. One only needs to glance at his commanding stature to see this.

"When I was 16 or 17 years old, I worked with a pulley mechanism designed to help astronauts combat atrophied muscles while in weightlessness," he confessed once. "I strengthened the muscles in my arms and legs, particularly my arms, to improve acceleration." This is why I can impart more spin on the ball with my topspin than any other player on the tour."

Rafa's left arm suffers greatly as a result of the topspin, particularly the rotator cuff muscle in his left shoulder. As a result, Rafa works hard to keep this particular area of his body in good working order. He claims to conduct far less jogging training than other top male players, fearing that doing so would harm his already strained body. His fitness trainer has previously noted that the majority of his running consists of sprint training in order to prepare for the abrupt changes in speed and direction around the tennis court.

Training in the water, where the pressure on his muscles and joints is less severe, is another favourite. The BOSU board (or wobble board) is a gym gadget that aids in footwork and balance. Before and after each workout, there is always a lot of stretching. Rafa, like many tennis players, uses ice baths after strenuous workouts (and even matches) to minimize inflammation and prepare his body for the next round of torture. Even in the early 2000s, fellow player Andre Agassi warned of impending bodily difficulties. "Nadal is signing cheques that one can only hope his body will be able to pay," he explained. "He works hard for every point, and you can only hope he stays healthy, but there's a lot of wear and tear." A great career is determined not only by what he can do, but also by his health." All professional tennis players will sustain an injury at some point in their careers. The most dedicated compete in up to 30 events every year, pounding, bruising, and hurting their bodies week after week. Granted, they have access to some of the best physiotherapists on the planet, but with such debilitating wear and strain, something has to give.

Rafa's first significant injury occurred in his left foot. It all started in 2004, when a stress fracture forced him to miss the majority of the clay-court season, including Roland Garros, due to a stress fracture. The same foot flared up again the next year. This time was far more serious. Rafa's doctor, Angel Cotorro, was unable to provide an acceptable diagnosis, so he sought the advice of a specialist in Madrid. Rafa had a congenital foot condition caused by a little bone in his foot (the tarsal scaphoid) that had failed to form properly during his youth. After years of tennis, the bone distorted, got larger, and was at risk of splintering. As a result, the tremendous pain.

Rafa was then given the worst possible news: he might never play competitive tennis again, according to the specialist. Rafa burst into tears. He felt as though his life had been slashed in half. Rafa's family rallied around him, like they always do. Toni urged his nephew to continue practising despite having to whack balls while sitting in a chair or standing on crutches. Rafa's father was still hopeful that they would find a solution. Rafa's shoe sponsors, Nike, eventually succeeded in manufacturing a shoe with extra padding on the sole to protect the fractured bone under the supervision of the Madrid specialist. He had to modify his playing style continuously to adapt the new boots, but it eventually worked. There was still some discomfort, but it was manageable. "We must arm ourselves to resist," he subsequently added. "Because there is no other solution than to resist."

Rafa had a fresh perspective on his career as a result of the entire experience. After coming so close to losing his favourite vocation, he resolved to tackle each and every match as if it were his last. His left foot wasn't his only issue. Over time, more injuries would occur: legs, shoulder, knees, wrist, hip, back, and fingers. He was more prone to knee ailments as a result of the specialised footwear, yet he needed the adapted tennis shoe to play.

The doping allegations

It was known as Operación Puerto. Spanish authorities initiated an investigation into a suspected sports doping network involving some of the world's top cyclists and cycling teams in the mid-2000s. In the midst of the chaos, one European publication reported that the doctor at the centre of the affair, Eufemiano Fuentes (who was later cleared of all charges), had a client list that included Rafa Nadal.

Rafa instantly asserted his innocence and denied any involvement in doping despite the lack of proof against him. Unfortunately, the seed of mistrust was set, and other tennis players disseminated false rumours about him using performance-enhancing substances in following years. Roselyne Bachelot, the country's minister for health and sports, went one step farther. In a TV appearance in 2016, she publicly accused him of doping. Rafa later sued her for defamation, saying that her statements harmed his reputation, and was granted 12,000 euros, which he donated to charity.

"I intended to defend not only my integrity and image as an athlete, but also the values I have defended throughout my career," Rafa remarked following the court ruling. "I also want to prevent any public figure from making false or insulting allegations against an athlete in the media without any evidence or foundation and going unpunished."

It is critical to emphasise that there has never been a scrap of evidence to suggest Rafa is guilty of doping. He has always maintained his innocence. "I am a completely clean guy," he told the Los Angeles Times in an interview. "I've worked so hard my entire career, and when I get hurt, I get hurt." I never take anything just to get back faster. And there was never any urge to do something bad. I believe in the sport and the principles it represents. It serves as a model for the children. If I do something that contradicts that, I will be deceiving myself, not my opponents."

The International Tennis Federation manages testing for performance-enhancing drugs as part of its Tennis Anti-Doping Programme. It is applicable to all players competing at the highest levels of tennis, including the Grand Slams, the ATP circuit, the WTA tour, and the Olympics. Without prior warning, players are required to submit to urine or blood tests at any time, in or out of competition. Furthermore, players ranked in the top 100 in the world must notify testers of their whereabouts every day of the year that they are not participating. In most years, only a few players are found to have violated doping rules.

Nadal, Rafael

Tennis at the Olympic Games is rarely of the highest calibre. When players strive to complete what is known as the Golden Slam: all four Grand Slam singles titles as well as the Olympic singles gold medal in the same calendar year, it makes for very fascinating viewing. Of course, this opportunity only comes up every four years, adding to its rarity.

Rafa has never had a chance to complete the Grand Slam. Only one player, Steffi Graf, has ever done so. Rafa has yet to win all four Grand Slam singles titles in the same calendar year (dubbed "The Calendar Slam" in the sport). He didn't give up hope, however, and won Roland Garros, Wimbledon, and the US Open in 2010.

Nonetheless, his 2008 Olympic gold medal match deserves special note, if only because it provided Rafa with the points he needed to end Federer's four-and-a-half-year reign at the top.

On that hot August day in 2008, when second-seeded Rafa and his 12th-seeded Chilean competitor Fernando Gonzalez found themselves on opposite sides of the net on the main court at Beijing's Olympic Green Tennis Centre, it was the latter who might have felt more assured. He has won both of the prior hard-court encounters between the two. Both players had performed admirably in the draw. Gonzalez, who had the seemingly easier path to the final, didn't drop a set until the semi-finals, when he was pushed to an 11-9 win in the deciding third set against American James Blake. Meanwhile, Rafa dropped a set in his nerve-wracking opening encounter, then another in the semi-finals against Djokovic.

Rafa, dressed in long white shorts, a dark-orange sleeveless top (with a tiny Spanish badge across the left breast), a light-orange headband, and supports across either knee, got the match started in typical brutal fashion, firing his first serve down the T and then killing Gonzalez's subsequent return with a massive forehand. The Chilean, dressed in a more conventional black and white tennis uniform, appeared nervous. He had one of the most powerful forehands in the world at the time... and he used it to great effect on occasion. However, not on this particular day. And, as all opponents know, it just takes a slight gap in your armour for Rafa to rip it open savagely.

Rafa stormed to a 3-0 lead in the first set, eventually winning 6-3. The most entertaining set, though, was the second, when Gonzalez manoeuvred himself into a double-set point position with a stunning, unreturnable inside-out forehand into the advantage service box. Having worked so hard to gain this advantage, he then blew both set points, the first by pushing an easy volley wide and the second by slamming a forehand into the net.

These blunders strained his nerves even more, causing him to make three forehand errors in the ensuing tiebreak. The Spaniard ultimately won handily, 7-2.

Rafa was in command from then on, breaking serve to love in the fourth game to take a 3-1 lead. Gonzalez fought valiantly, as the squeaking of both players' shoes on the DecoTurf hard court became more audible. But Gonzalez's efforts were futile, as his opponent went on to win the match and the Olympic gold medal by closing off the set 6-3.

Later, at the medal presentation, Rafa received his medal from fellow Spaniard Juan Antonio Samaranch while dressed in an ill-fitting Spain tracksuit. Gonzales won silver, while Djokovic got bronze after defeating James Blake in the third-place play-off match. Yes, Rafa did bite his gold medal, as he does every award he receives. Finally, he posed for the photographers, wearing the Spanish flag as a cape.

"I know how difficult it is to win these things, especially here, because you only have one chance every four years," he stated at the post-match press conference. "Grand Slams are more important in tennis than they are here." But in this town, you only get one chance every four years. The problem is, when I win here, I feel like I've won for the entire country. Isn't that more unique? I win for a lot of people, not just myself."

Later, he reconsidered the significance of his victory. "It's an honour to be a part of the Olympic family of Spanish sport," he remarked. "What I experienced during the Olympic Games was unforgettable; it's something you won't find on the tour, not even in a Grand Slam." That was one of the most memorable experiences of my life."

Perhaps the most significant part of Rafa's Olympic victory was how it later enabled him to accomplish what is known as the career Golden Slam: a gold medal plus victories in all four Grand Slams at any point in one's career. Only two men have done so to date: Rafa and Andre Agassi.

CHAPTER 6

FAME IN SPAIN

"For the first time in my career, I played a very, very good match in this tournament. That's my feeling, no? I played my best match in the US Open at the most important moment."

Rafa Nadal, after the 2010 US Open

Is Rafael Nadal the most well-known Spanish athlete of all time? He is without a doubt the most well-known Spanish tennis player. There have only been five world number one singles players from Spain during the Open Era (from 1968, when tennis became professional, to the current day): Rafa, Carlos Moya (who is now Rafa's coach), Juan Carlos Ferrero, Arantxa Sánchez Vicario, and Garbie Muguruza.

But keep in mind that there are world number ones and world number ones. Rafa has held the number one place for a total of 209 weeks (no other Spaniard comes close), and he has 21 Grand Slam victories to his name. Moya, Ferrero, Sánchez Vicario, and Muguruza, on the other hand, have only eight Grand Slam championships between them. (There is also one Spaniard from before the Open Era worth mentioning: Manuel Santana, who won Wimbledon, the US Open, and Roland Garros twice in the 1960s.)

But what about other sports? There are many renowned bullfighters and pelota players from Spain throughout history, but due to the nature of their games, they encountered minimal foreign competition. It wasn't until General Franco's death in 1975, Spain's subsequent route to democracy (in the early 1980s), and its admission to the European Union (in 1986) that the country began to properly exercise its sporting muscles. Tennis players, golfers, footballers, basketball players, cyclists, and race drivers were able to shine as a result of the economic success founded on political stability.

Perhaps the most powerful driver of all was Spain's successful bid for the Olympic Games, which it hosted in Barcelona in 1992. That summer felt gloriously bright and upbeat for Spaniards and the rest of the globe watching as 169 nations and nearly 10,000 athletes flocked to the Catalan capital to compete. It was the first Summer Olympics held after the Cold War's end, with several former Soviet and Yugoslav nations competing under their newly independent flags. After a 32-year ban, South Africa was welcomed. For the first time since the 1960s, Germany sent a cohesive squad. Riding the tide of enthusiasm and taking advantage of their home advantage, Spanish competitors won a total of 22 medals, including 13 golds, ranking them sixth overall in the medal table.

Around the remainder of that decade, the Spanish government built sports training facilities around the country. The public and the media jumped on board, enthusiastically supporting their new sporting heroes. Hundreds of sports benefited from government investment at the grassroots level.

Suddenly, the entire world became aware of new Spanish champions. We witnessed Cesc Fàbregas, Iker Casillas, David Villa, Sergio Ramos, Fernando Torres, Gerard Piqué, Xavi Hernández, Ral González, Carles Puyol, and Andrés Iniesta in football. Spain won the World Cup in 2010 (with Rafa in the dressing room to celebrate), as well as the Euros in 2008 and 2012.

Spaniards lit up golf courses as well, beginning with Seve Ballesteros and continuing with Sergio Garcia, José Mariá Olazábal (with whom Rafa has organised a charity golf tournament), Miguel Angel Jiménez, and John Rahm.

Fernando Alonso won the Formula One world championship twice for Renault, in 2005 and 2006, and came close to winning it again for Ferrari. Marc Marquez has won the MotoGP title six times. Miguel Indurain has won the Tour de France five times.

It is impossible to compare the athletic achievements of a tennis player to those of a race driver or a golfer to those of a basketball player. You may compare oranges and lemons in the centre of an orchard in Andalucia in the middle of the day. How could you possibly place Grand Slam tennis victories alongside Formula One race victories? How do weeks at the top of the ATP world rankings compare to being awarded La Liga champion club several times?

Despite these evident issues with sport analytics, Rafa still shines brighter than all of his contemporaries in all of their sports, no matter how you evaluate his success: 21 Grand Slam singles championships; 69 ATP titles; two Olympic gold medals (one singles, one doubles); five Davis Cup team victories; 209 weeks as world number one; five times as year-end world number one.

Marca, Spain's main sports newspaper, asked its readers to vote for their country's greatest of all time, or GOAT, in 2020. "The Spanish GOAT battle," they called their knock-out poll of 16 renowned Spanish athletes (the majority of whom were mentioned above). Rafa was the clear winner by a wide margin.

"Spain has had no shortage of sporting glory in recent years, making it an almost impossible task to choose the standout star," the authors said. "However, after a battle to find the country's sporting GOAT, Rafa Nadal has taken the prize."

In a recent interview, another Spanish tennis player Alex Corretja elegantly summarised his colleague's success. "When Rafael Nadal wins, we all win," he stated sport.es after Rafa won his 20th Grand Slam championship in 2020. "It's tough for me to put into words what Rafa represents to all of us. He is, in my opinion, the greatest Spanish athlete of all time, with complete respect for everyone else. "I want to remember that Rafa is human, even if he acts like a machine; that he is sensitive, even if he has the appearance of iron; and that his game can be as overwhelming as lava from a volcano."

While the players frequently delivered at the top level, the tournament's television partners, CBS, fell short. Despite the fact that the final had already been moved from Sunday to Monday, and that another storm was brewing along the east coast, they insisted on a late start in order to capitalise on the early-evening viewing schedule and the commercial opportunities it provided. If they had chosen to hold the match earlier, it might have been over before the rain arrived.

The two competitors - Rafa in all black with fluorescent yellow shoes and Djokovic in white shirt and black shorts - began their encounter with vigour, taking almost 30 minutes to complete the opening five games. The first point was a long affair, contested over 19 shots. The second game rally at 30-all was even longer, lasting 28 strokes. By the fifth game of what was clearly going to be a huge slugfest, Djokovic had been required to defend no fewer than six breakpoints. Rafa let five of them go before unleashing a huge forehand winner. He then immediately went on to win the first set.

The Serbs upped the pace in the second set, rushing to a 4-1 lead, the metronomic interchange of grunting and squeaking of their shoes lending a weirdly mesmerising aspect to longer rallies. But Rafa fought back valiantly, tying the game at four games all, 30-all. The storm hit at that point, causing a roughly two-hour delay.

Rafa's best season was unquestionably 2010. He won the French Open, Wimbledon, and the US Open that year, becoming the only male player in tennis history to win Grand Slam singles titles on clay, grass, and hard courts in the same year.

Rafa, the world number one, arrived at the USTA Billie Jean King National Tennis Center in New York that year, brimming with enthusiasm and confidence. He hadn't dropped a single set all the way to the final. Djokovic, on the other hand, had to endure a gruelling five-set duel against Viktor Troicki in the opening round that lasted three hours and forty minutes. He had to work even harder in the semi-finals against Roger Federer, in another difficult five-setter that depleted his energy reserves. Despite this, the Serb was motivated to put up a good fight against Rafa. Indeed, it felt more like heavyweight boxing than tennis at moments.

Both players appeared to be much more fired up upon their comeback, playing with increased energy. That second set was closed out by the Serb.

If Rafa was disheartened by this, he didn't show it. He won the third set because of some incredible intensity. He broke Djokovic's service in the third game of the fourth set before sprinting to victory. Djokovic's final forehand went wide after three hours and 43 minutes. Nadal collapsed to the floor on his back before sliding around onto his front, head in hands, as if hit by a bullet. His emotions erupted, his back heaving up and down as he wept for joy.

Following that, he was asked to evaluate his biggest strengths as a player. "The mentality, the attitude on the court, I think it was always good for me," he remarked. "I am always upbeat and fighting on the court." When I'm playing well, my intensity is always high. The tempo is fast. I can keep playing at the same rhythm and level for a long period."

Djokovic was courteous to the winner. "It's fantastic for someone who has had as much success as he has, [at] such a young age, to be able to keep motivating himself to do his best at each tournament; each match he plays, regardless of who is across the net." You just have to tip your hat to this guy. Everything he does, both on and off the field. excellent champion, excellent person, and amazing athlete example."

But it was possibly the famed American coach Brad Gilbert who best summarised Rafa's effort that night. "Rafa's fortitude is just off the charts," he says. "He never gives up, whether it's 40-love up or 40-love down." He simply does not deduct a point."

CHAPTER 7

FAMILY

"The number of wins that he has made at Roland Garros is incredible. Each time you step on the court with him, you know that you have to climb Mount Everest to win against this guy here."

Novak Djokovic

Rafa and his family are more close than others in a country and on an island where family members are generally inseparable. To say they were close would be an understatement. This tennis player's bond with his parents, grandparents, aunts, uncles, nephews, nieces, and cousins - many of whom he has spent much of his life living cheek by jowl with - is extremely close. They almost operate as a single entity in terms of finances, emotions, psychology, and culture.

Rafa claims that for the majority of his life, his family life has been happy, stable, united, harmonious, and reassuringly familiar. When Rafa is happy, his entire extended family is happy. When he is sad, everyone is sad. The Nadals, as detailed in Chapter 6, are similar to the mafia but "without the malice or the guns."

So when his parents, Sebastián and Ana Maria, announced in 2009 that they were intending to divorce after nearly 30 years of marriage, the news was extremely upsetting for Rafa.

His father was the one who informed him that he and his mother were divorcing. On the plane home from the Australian Open, he told his son about his triumph over Federer. "Suddenly, and utterly without warning, the happy family portrait had cracked," he explained in his autobiography Rafa: My Story. "The continuity I valued in my life had been slashed in half, and the emotional order on which I rely had been dealt a devastating blow."

Initially, the impact on Rafa's tennis appeared minor. He won the Masters Series tournaments in Indian Wells, Monte Carlo, and Rome that spring. But by Roland Garros, the fractures in his stoic visage had begun to show. In Paris, he was defeated in the fourth round by Swedish player Robin Soderling. It remains one of only four defeats in his career in the French Open. His supremacy decreased as the season went, and a knee problem flared up, aggravated, he claimed, by the breakdown of his parents' relationship at home. That year, he didn't even make it to Wimbledon. To make matters worse, he tore an abdominal muscle during the North American hard-court swing. By August of that year, he had fallen from first to third in the world rankings. Granted, it wasn't a total tragedy in the broad scheme of things, but it was an indication of how parental conflict was impacting both his mind and body.

"My parents' divorce made an important change in my life," he subsequently remarked. "It had an impact on me." It was difficult after that since I couldn't play Wimbledon. I was out of the world for a month."

Fortunately, the rest of his family came to his aid. He realised he needed to shake himself out of his stupor by the end of 2009. He began to improve his fortunes after receiving professional therapy for his knee ailment (see Chapter 7).

In 2010, he won Roland Garros (revenge on Soderling), his second Wimbledon title, and his first US Open trophy. Rafa was back, and he was back with a vengeance.

There were rumours two years later that Sebastián and Ana Maria had resumed their relationship. Few people outside the family know for certain if this is true. It's more likely that they've simply agreed to put their disagreements aside and attend Rafa's events together, as they used to, in order to restore some stability to their son's tennis career.

There's little doubt that his support team and family were a lifeline during this difficult time. Maribel, in particular, was a source of comfort for him.

Maribel was busy creating her own business while Rafa was spending his scholastic years on the tennis court with Uncle Toni. She attended the Colegio Pureza de Mara, a prominent Catholic school in her family's hometown, as a child. It was here that she met Maria Francisca Perelló, or Mery, the girl she introduced to her brother and whom he subsequently married. Maribel studied sports science and management in Barcelona after high school, and business management in Palma de Mallorca. Later, she worked for sports and entertainment agency IMG (which had represented her brother), insurance company Mapfre (which was one of her brother's sponsors), and Banco Santander (which was another of her brother's sponsors). She is now mostly hired by her brother, who works in marketing for the Rafa Nadal Academy. This may appear to be nepotistic, but it demonstrates the Nadal family's close-knit business.

Mery, Rafa's wife, is another of his employees. Despite the fact that she is married to one of the world's most famous athletes, little is known about her. She is an incredibly secretive person who practically never agrees to be interviewed, which has given her an almost cryptic, mythological personality. Her privacy has never been compromised, thanks to the uncommon Mallorcan habit of giving superstars the space they require. If she and Rafa had lived anywhere else in Europe, the tabloid press and paparazzi would have relentlessly pursued them. It's another reason the pair has never left their island home.

Mery only does interviews on very rare occasions, and the questions are addressed by email, disclosing nothing personal. Even in Rafa's book, she is only referenced for a few lines, blandly saying that she prefers not to travel with Rafa and that she finds the realm of public stardom "asphyxiating."

She was born in Manacor in 1988, the only daughter of Bernat, who managed an estate agency, and Mara, who worked as a civil servant at the municipal council. A quick word about her name: the Spanish and worldwide press have nicknamed her Xisca, although Rafa and his family refer to her as Mery or Mary - both spellings are used. "I have many names," she recently told the Spanish edition of Vanity Fair magazine. "My friends and family call me Mery. It was in the news that they first referred to me as Xisca. Nobody calls me that, and that is the name with which I am least familiar."

Rafa was quite bashful around girls when he was little. It was his sister who encouraged Mery and her brother's friendship. She is the only serious girlfriend he has ever had, as far as anyone knows.

After 14 years as boyfriend and girlfriend, the couple married in October 2019 at the Sa Fortaleza estate in Pollença, a town on the island's northern shore. The estate, which was originally a 17th-century fort designed to defend Mallorca from pirates, was featured in the BBC version of John Le Carré's The Night Manager.

The Nadal family, ever modest, wanted to avoid the pomp and formality of a famous wedding. However, inviting past Spanish monarchs Juan Carlos I and Queen Sofia did nothing to dampen the excitement. Other tennis players on the 200-person guest list included Feliciano López, Carlos Moya, David Ferrer, Juan Mónaco, and their partners.

Mery, a University of the Balearic Islands graduate in business management, is now the director of her husband's children's charity, the Rafa Nadal Foundation. Her job requires her to travel to India at least once a year to the foundation's school (the Nadal Educational

Tennis School) in Anantapur, in the country's south. "I remember very well the impact it had on me the first time I was in Anantapur," she explained to Vanity Fair. "Their reality is so different from ours. It is tough to articulate what their life expectations and priorities are. I was astounded to see how much the kids at school value the clothes and shoes we provide them. They treasure them and keep them in their houses."

Mery maintains a modest profile despite her charitable endeavours. She rarely travels to her husband's tournaments, except at key periods in his career when she'll appear with Maribel and Ana Maria, and she always remains quiet and out of the spotlight. And Rafa prefers it that way. "We've known each other forever, since we were little," he once said. "Mery is a source of comfort for me."

Thirteen may be unlucky for most people, but not for Rafa in the autumn of 2020 at Roland Garros. In a Covid-delayed French Open final, he defeated Novak Djokovic in three sets, taking only two hours and 41 minutes to win his 13th Roland Garros championship and 20th Grand Slam overall.

In actuality, the scoreline - 6-0, 6-2, 7-5 - belied the calibre of resistance that Djokovic faced on that cool day in Paris. With the exception of a default at the US Open, where he was penalised for mistakenly striking a ball into the throat of a line judge, Djokovic had not lost a match all year. Granted, the season had been significantly shortened due to the global pandemic. Nonetheless, the Serb was in superb condition heading into the final.

But not breathtaking enough for Rafa. The Spaniard, dressed in a baby blue shirt and shorts with a bright red headband, won the first set 6-0 in 45 minutes. This is known as a bagel in tennis. It was a humiliation for a player of Djokovic's stature. It wasn't that he didn't play well; it was just that Rafa was too damn good. He'd been too good for the entire tournament, dropping only one set on his path to triumph.

The match had a melancholy tinge to it, with only a thousand paying fans at the Court Philippe Chatrier, all wearing protective face masks. Rain forced the stadium's new retractable roof to close, marking the first time the French Open final had been played under cover in its 130-year history. The echoes of the balls striking the rackets, as well as the grunts of both players as they laboured through the rest of the match, were intensified.

Rafa easily won the second set as well, his serve placement often pinpoint-perfect. Djokovic, for his part, continued to make unforced errors. Dropshots were used repeatedly by the Serb to try to trip up his opponent. Some worked, while others did not. "I obviously wanted to disrupt his rhythm," he explained after the match. "But he was prepared. He was there, and he was ready."

By the third set, Djokovic had managed to put up more of a fight. Following an early break of his own, he broke Rafa's serve for the first time in the match, marking the occasion with a fist-clenched yell.

The Serb found himself break point behind again after five games. He took a chance and hit his serve near the line. It appeared to be in at first, but after the chair umpire checked the mark in the clay, it was called out for a double fault.

This proved too much for Djokovic psychologically. Rafa then served out his final game to love, hitting his final ace wide to his opponent's backhand, so wide that the Serb could only watch helplessly as it passed him by. Rafa then went to his knees instead of collapsing on his back, which was rare for a success celebration. He jumped back up to sympathise with his opponent, pointing his fingers and pumping his arms with a gaping smile. When he returned to the centre of the court, he clutched his shirt with both hands and bit it between his teeth, as if he couldn't believe he'd won. This was his 100th Roland Garros match. What a great way to win.

With so few people in attendance, the prize ceremony was rather quiet. Rafa and Djokovic had covered their faces with masks by this point, so Rafa couldn't bite his trophy right away, though he could and did near the end of the presentation runway.

"Today you showed why you are king of the clay," the vanquished told the victor, with all due respect.

"A win here means everything to me," Rafa added. I've spent most of my career's pivotal times here. Simply playing here is an inspiration, and my love story with this city and this court is unforgettable."

The magnitude of Rafa's 20th Grand Slam astounded BBC pundit David Law. "I didn't know if he had that level of tennis in him at the age of 34," he explained. "It's been 15 years since he won this thing." He's in his 30s and plays really devastating tennis. Novak Djokovic was built to fail. Rafael Nadal could not have been stopped by two players today, in my opinion. The fact that he has drawn level with Roger Federer is a watershed moment in the sport."

Guy Forget was the tournament director at Roland Garros. "It's just beyond anything that anyone could have imagined," he remarked of the game. "Perhaps someone will witness something better in the future, but in my opinion, that is the greatest sporting achievement any sport will ever see."

CHAPTER 8

WHAT LIES AHEAD

"In Mallorca, I can be myself. I go to the supermarket and the cinema, and I am just Rafa. Everyone knows me, and it is no big deal. I can go all day – no photographs."

Rafa Nadal

When astronomers name an asteroid after you, you know you're renowned. The Astronomical Observatory of Mallorca spotted a four-kilometre-diameter asteroid racing around our solar system in 2003. They initially assigned it the number 128036. After Rafa won his first Wimbledon title five years later, they made an official request to the International Astronomical Union to rename it in honour of their island's most famous son.

As a result, this massive rock racing through our solar system at a pace of 20 kilometres per second is now known as the Rafael Nadal asteroid.

A more traditional memorial to this great champion can be located at Stade Roland Garros in Paris, the location of so many of his greatest triumphs. In May 2021, a massive statue of Rafa was unveiled close to the complex's new general public entrance gate, near the Jardin des Mousquetaires, with the player himself in attendance. The statue, which stands three metres tall and is made of stainless steel, depicts the Mallorcan as he follows through on one of his tremendous forehands.

It's the work of Jordi Dez Fernandez, a Spanish sculptor who was there when his artwork was unveiled. "What I want to express with the sculpture is a synthesis of all his attributes, which can perhaps be boiled down to just one: strength," Fernandez said. "I created a sculpture of Rafa Nadal that projects his strength." In reality, it is a monument to human strength."

The artist recalls being taken aback by Rafa's physical presence the first time he met him. "He has the proportions of a professional athlete." But the truth is that he's incredibly down-to-earth, humble, and personable from the start. Rafa Nadal, in my opinion, is an icon, an inspiration to all of us. When we watch Rafa play, we see all of these attributes in him that motivate us to discover our own potential."

Gilles Moretton, head of the French Tennis Federation, presided over the unveiling of the statue. "Rafa, your name has been associated with Roland Garros since 2005," he remarked, paying respect to the 13-time French Open champion. "You've written, and continue to write, wonderful history for both the tournament and yourself."

History is a highly valued idea in a sport like tennis, which dates back to the 1870s. Tennis enthusiasts and players, like many other well-established sports, can become slightly obsessed with historical playing records. And there is one record that is widely regarded as the most important: the overall number of Grand Slam singles titles.

As this book was being written, Rafa had 21 Grand Slams, one more than his two greatest opponents, Roger Federer and Novak Djokovic. Rafa won two Australian Opens, thirteen French Opens, two Wimbledons, and four United States Opens. Meanwhile, Djokovic has won nine Australian Opens, two French Opens, six Wimbledons, and three US Opens. Federer won six Australian Opens, one French Open, eight Wimbledons, and five US Opens over his career.

We should consider ourselves fortunate to be living in such a golden age of tennis achievement. At no other time in the history of the sport have three male competitors developed such a competitive, entertaining, and compelling competition. Only five other men (Pete Sampras, Roy Emerson, Bjorn Borg, Rod Laver, and Bill Tilden) have won ten or more Grand Slam titles in the sport's history. (In the women's game, three players have won more than 20 Grand Slam singles titles: Steffi Graf with 22, Serena Williams with 23, and Margaret Court with 24.)

Most players try to downplay the significance of winning numerous Grand Slams. It's a psychological strategy they use to avoid feeling burdened by the weight of all this history, as well as an effort to focus on the now rather than worrying about future matches. But the truth is that for the best players, it's always a goal at the back of their thoughts, and sometimes in the front.

Tennis' Grand Slam total has been an interest for American sports journalists in particular. It corresponds to the broader concept of "greatest of all time," or GOAT. Experts and amateurs alike argue constantly about who the GOAT is in each sport and what results qualify them for that honour. In tennis, however, debating GOAT designation is useless because the number of Grand Slam singles championships is so clearly defined. Rafa is still evasive on the matter. "I have never hidden the fact that I would like to retire as the best in history, and as the player with the most Grand Slams," he stated in a 2021 interview with Spanish newspaper El Pais. But I'm not going to stress over it. It's not that I don't want to put myself under strain. I express what I think: I'd like to end my career this way. Of course, it's a goal for me, but it's not something I'm obsessed with. "My main goal is to be satisfied with what I do. "Then, after winning his 21st Grand Slam at the Australian Open in January 2022, surpassing Federer and Djokovic, he commented, "At the end, it doesn't matter much if one is 21, the other is 20." Alternatively, one can finish with 23 or 21. We did significant things for our sport, attained our goals, and had fun doing it. "I consider myself fortunate to have been a part of this historic era in our sport."

Rafa and Djokovic are still in their thirties. If their bodies hold up, they could both play for another five years. Consider Federer, who is currently in his sixth decade. Although the Swiss champion will not admit it, there is just one aim that keeps him on court, and that is to win more Grand Slams than his two opponents. If you could look into the souls of all three participants, you might find out what genuinely inspires them all.

What does this trio's future hold? Federer will almost certainly have to retire soon due to his ageing body. Djokovic appears to have plenty of fire left in his belly and, on paper, has the best chance of adding to his Grand Slam record - though his stance on Covid vaccines may limit his ambition somewhat. But what about the man we're most curious about? What can we anticipate from Rafa?

When asked recently when he planned to retire, he was predictably tight-lipped. "I'm not sure. Tennis is a mental game. It's not a mathematical problem. I'll know when the time arrives."

When that day comes, there will be plenty to keep the man busy. For example, all of the Nadal family's economic interests. As well as the Rafa Nadal Tennis Academy. He recently stated that he wishes to devote his time to his humanitarian foundation, the Rafa Nadal Foundation, which assists impoverished youngsters.

What about his own children? While there is no danger of future Nadals becoming impoverished, Rafa has always stated that he would wait until he retired from professional tennis before starting a family with his wife Mery. She is, however, in her mid-30s. Tennis and fatherhood may overlap if he continues to play for a few more years.

"I am a very family-oriented person," he told the Argentine newspaper La Nacion in an interview. "You never know what will happen in the future, but I know I'm going to start a family." I intend to have children. I'm not sure how many. I adore children, but making a decision is something that requires two people. I'd like to have multiple children, but I'm not sure if it'll be two, three, or four."

Rafa has stated that he will always judge his success in terms of his personal and family life, rather than money or tournament trophies. "Real success is having friends and family, taking care of them, and feeling loved by others, especially the public." But feeling loved by people close to you is even more vital."

When asked about his tennis legacy, Rafa says he would rather be known as a great guy than a great tennis player. "In the end, sport will always exist." What you have accomplished will be preserved. However, when [your work] comes to an end, you will be treated for the legacy you have left behind. That legacy is made up of the friends you've made on the circuit and how nicely you've treated the people of the world. And I hope that has been something I have been mindful of over the years. I believe it is. People appreciate me wherever I go, both the tournament organisers and the people on the circuit with whom I intend to stay in touch."

Rafa has accomplished so much in his 21-year career that it's breathtaking. On the court, he has won 21 Grand Slam singles titles, 69 ATP titles, the career Golden Slam, two Olympic gold medals, five Davis Cup team victories, 209 weeks ranked number one in the world, five times finishing the year ranked number one, and 81 consecutive wins on clay, the longest single-surface winning streak in Open Era history.

Off the court, we should recognize his academy and philanthropic organisation. Granted, he was always too busy competing to put in the effort to develop these, but they are nonetheless significant accomplishments.

Looking back, he realises how fortunate he has been thus far. "I consider myself fortunate in life because of everything that has happened to me and everything I now have." I do things for fun, and I thank everyone who loves me from all around the world. They are truly lovely things, and I can only thank God for them."

Was it his most impressive comeback? Rafa undoubtedly thought so after rallying from two sets down in the 2022 Australian Open final to capture his record 21st Grand Slam singles title. So did the majority of his devoted fans in Rod Laver Arena.

The effort and physicality he demonstrated on that Melbourne court in the heat and humidity was amazing enough. When you consider the flaws in his preparation for the Australian Open, his accomplishment shines even brighter.

It was unclear whether the 35-year-old would even compete. He had been out for the majority of the previous six months due to a chronic foot injury that had necessitated surgery. This had reduced his match practice and impeded his training. He had even worried that he would never compete again. The Covid infection then struck him down just a few weeks before the competition, significantly delaying his preparation.

Despite this, he arrived in Melbourne as the sixth seed and in surprisingly good form. He only dropped one set in the first four rounds. Then he was put to the test: his quarter-final battle against Denis Shapovalov went to five sets, and his semi-final encounter against Matteo Berrettini went to four sets. So, when his Russian opponent Daniil Medvedev - 10 years his junior - stormed to a two-sets-to-love lead in the final, fans were sympathetic. It appeared that the game had ended.

But, as we've all learned over the years, Rafa is never out of the game. This is undoubtedly the most tenacious, unyielding player to ever take the court. Even when he's at his lowest point, he's never out.

Rafa needed to use all of his superpowers to turn the match around after Medvedev led 6-2, 7-6. In the sixth game of the third set, he faced three break points, which proved decisive. He defeated all three.

The Spaniard then recognized his moment to attack in the eighth game. Rafa broke serve and then took the set after Medvedev missed an easy volley. It provided the groundwork for his eventual return.

Tension rose dramatically throughout the fourth set, which had 15 break points. Rafa won two of them, setting up a crucial fifth set.

He executed some very brilliant sliced backhands and dropshots while frequently coming closer to the baseline to pressurise his opponent. There's no doubt he was aided by his vocally partisan supporters, who were at times aggressive in their applause for Medvedev's unforced errors. The Russian was clearly shaken, even pleading with the umpire to reprimand the more rowdy players.

Rafa finally served out the final game to love following a five-hour and twenty-four-minute fight. He shook his head in disbelief at what he had accomplished: a masterstroke; the greatest of great escapes.

"It's just amazing - the way it happened is even more unique," he stated later. "This has been, without a doubt, one of the most special titles of my career, because coming back after six months without playing and not knowing if my foot can hold a professional match at all, and being able to compete that way, is something unexpected and a big surprise for me."

He characterised himself as "physically destroyed." Emotions were also running high. So high, in fact, that he couldn't sleep the night after the match.

"I feel lucky to have achieved one more very special thing in my tennis career," he stated after receiving his 21st Grand Slam trophy. "I don't care if I'm the one or not; if I'm the best in history or not the best in history."

But that was just me being modest. The bright smile on his face demonstrated that this struggle with Roger Federer and Novak Djokovic to be the best of all time is one he is keen to win.

Congratulations poured in from all directions. "A final of Herculean proportions," remarked Australian tennis icon Rod Laver, who presented the trophy to the Spaniard. "This historic victory is so special, Rafa, given everything you've been through." It's been a pleasure to watch you accomplish what you love."

Billie Jean King, the former American champion, was likewise astounded. "The mental and physical marathon of a five-hour Grand Slam final requires grit, guts, spirit, and determination," she explained. "What an amazing comeback!"

Federer was evidently awestruck by his opponent. "What a match!" he exclaimed. "My heartfelt congratulations to my friend and great rival on becoming the first man to win 21 Grand Slam singles titles." Amazing. A great champion should never be underestimated. Your remarkable work ethic, dedication, and battling spirit inspire me and millions others worldwide."

The contents of this book may not be copied, reproduced or transmitted without the express written permission of the author or publisher. Under no circumstances will the publisher or author be responsible or liable for any damages, compensation or monetary loss arising from the information contained in this book, whether directly or indirectly. .

Disclaimer Notice:

Although the author and publisher have made every effort to ensure the accuracy and completeness of the content, they do not, however, make any representations or warranties as to the accuracy, completeness, or reliability of the content. , suitability or availability of the information, products, services or related graphics contained in the book for any purpose. Readers are solely responsible for their use of the information contained in this book

Every effort has been made to make this book possible. If any omission or error has occurred unintentionally, the author and publisher will be happy to acknowledge it in upcoming versions.

Made in United States
Cleveland, OH
12 January 2025